INSIDE INTELLIGENCE

INSIDE
INTELLIGENCE

Anthony Cavendish

COLLINS
London · 1990

William Collins Sons & Co. Ltd
London · Glasgow · Sydney · Auckland
Toronto · Johannesburg

First published privately 1987

This edition first published 1990

Copyright © Anthony Cavendish 1987
Copyright in introduction © Anthony Cavendish 1990

BRITISH LIBRARY CATALOGUING IN PUBLICATION DATA

Cavendish, Anthony
Inside intelligence.
1. British intelligence services. History. – Biographies
I. Title
327.12092

ISBN 0–00–215742–X

Photoset in Linotron Sabon by
J&L Composition Ltd, Filey, North Yorkshire
Printed and bound in Great Britain by
Hartnolls Ltd, Bodmin, Cornwall

For Elspeth, Julius and Charlotte

ACKNOWLEDGEMENTS

In writing about the activities of the Secret Service I have no desire to cause embarrassment to former officers of the intelligence services still living, and I have sought not to cause any embarrassment to those who were active in the Service and whose membership has remained a secret even from their families.

Four books which blow a vast hole in the cover of SIS have been particularly helpful to me in establishing exact dates and places for my memories: Kim Philby's *My Silent War* (1968), Jonathan Bloch and Patrick Fitzgerald's *British Intelligence and Covert Action* (1983), Anthony Verrier's *Through the Looking Glass* (1983), and Nigel West's *MI6* (1983). Unfortunately, these books leave many questions unanswered but they do open to the public gaze a great deal of what was previously tightly closed.

This book would not have been written without the encouragement of my wife, who told me I owed it to my two young children to tell them something of my early life.

I have spoken to old friends in MI6 who have helped me and I salute them.

And I thank Lynda Lamerton who took the whole thing down from my dictation and produced the finished manuscript.

FOREWORD

by George Young, ex-Deputy Chief MI6

Anthony Cavendish's narration spans a crucial phase in the development of British intelligence. It draws on his personal experience and on his long friendship with the Director General of MI6, the late Sir Maurice Oldfield. *Inside Intelligence* comes out at an apposite time. For the belief is again current in Whitehall – and Westminster – that putting an outside man in charge of the Secret Services will bring them under better control and curb their alleged 'wild men'. In fact, the opposite happens. The outsider knows neither the qualities of the individuals in the Service nor how in their daily routine work the events arise which determine their decisions. As happened with Major General Sir John Sinclair – who succeeded the legendary Stewart Menzies, to ensure that military intelligence was given proper priority – the outsider was totally lost. His orders bore no relation to reality so that they were ignored on the working level; sometimes with successful outcome as in setting the stage for the overthrow of Mossadeqh, and sometimes disastrously as with frogman Crabbe. In the case of the Baltic operations described by the author, Sinclair ignored repeated warnings that these were in the KGB's control. Under Sir John Rennie, imposed on the Service by the Foreign and Commonwealth Office, intelligence collection ground to a halt, morale sank to zero and security suffered.

There was general relief when Maurice Oldfield took over as 'C' in 1973. Oldfield was essentially a desk man whose forte was assessing and collating information supplied by others, but at least he encouraged field officers to get on with the job. During the 1950s when he ran Far Eastern operations, his main achievement was keeping in perspective the fluid and turbulent situation in South-East Asia after the French withdrawal and stressing that personal ambitions and tribal loyalties lay behind the upsets, coups and intrigues and not the hand of either Moscow or Peking.

If Britain did not get dragged into that costly and bloody intervention, as happened to the Americans, this is in no small part due to the effect of Oldfield's balanced assessments, worked out with Sir Robert Scott, Commissioner General for South-East Asia. The Far East reports were regular lead-in items in the weekly summary sent in the famous yellow box to the Prime Minister. The CIA officers in the Far East fully respected Oldfield's judgement and it is one of the tragedies of history that their views were overruled in Washington, where academic 'hawks' – and how hawkish they can be – acquired a complete ascendancy over the naïve Kennedy.

In the 1960s and 1970s the Middle East situation became ever more chaotic and the Foreign Office appreciations and guidance began to look increasingly irrelevant. Oldfield's contacts – established when he began his intelligence career as a Field Security sergeant – not only became indispensable sources of information but valuable points of influence, such as Teddy Kollek, the 'perpetual' mayor of Jerusalem.

This did not only apply in the Middle East. Unlike previous 'C's, Oldfield enjoyed travelling round the world and exchanging views with the heads of allied and friendly (not always the same thing!) intelligence services such as the West German *Bundesnachrichtendienst*, the French DEC, the Shah's SAVAK and the formidable South African BOSS. When the archives one day are opened, we will be able to gauge how influential Oldfield was in overcoming the Cabinet Office dislike of hard facts which would conflict with its preference for soothing description. The Falklands war is an example of where the latter prevailed at a high price. At the time of the EOKA B attempted coup in Cyprus in 1974, Oldfield played a vital role in cooling down Turkish fury over the tergiversations of Wilson and Callaghan.

The wounds inflicted on the SIS/CIA relationship by the Philby affair took a long time to heal. The CIA's counterespionage expert, Jim Angleton – a gullible soul who saw himself as a Machiavelli – had been completely under Philby's influence and sought to whitewash himself by finding KGB agents in every

British department and agency. As SIS Liaison Officer in Washington from 1960 to 1962, Oldfield tactfully coped with this, aided by the fact that most of his CIA Far East friends had by then been posted to senior jobs in the agency while Angleton's obsessions gradually brought him into ridicule and eventually the sack. Given the importance of US technical intelligence for NATO strategy, the value of his restoring American confidence in the British Services cannot be over-emphasized.

As 'C' from 1973 to 1978, Oldfield successfully resisted Wilson's attempts to embroil SIS in his domestic political intrigues and coped with David Owen's penchant for playing off Foreign Office against the intelligence services. Oldfield deserved something better than Mrs Thatcher's cold, noncommittal statement in the Commons on 23 April 1987. The achievements of 'C' may have of necessity to go unsung: they should not be distorted by a *faux bourdon*.

LONDON, 1990

INTRODUCTION

In July 1989 five Law Lords sitting as the highest Court of Appeal in the land rejected the Government's appeal to prevent newspapers reproducing extracts from this book. A battle, which had gone on for over two years, had apparently come to an end.

National newspapers published several editorials supporting me, but I like none better than Richard Ingrams's column in the *Observer* (9 July 1989).

Last week, the Law Lords finally ruled that Mr Anthony Cavendish, the former MI6 officer, was free to publish his memoirs. I first met Cavendish at the memorial service in 1975 for our mutual friend Sefton Delmer, the legendary *Daily Express* foreign correspondent who masterminded the Black Propaganda Radio during the war.

Later, as editor of *Private Eye*, I was able, with Cavendish's support, to defend Delmer's name against allegations that he had been a Communist agent – a preposterous charge against a man easily as right-wing as Cavendish himself.

Cavendish, in an old-fashioned way, feels obliged to defend the memory of his friends, which is why he was later so keen to publish his memoirs, in this case to speak up for the late Sir Maurice Oldfield. According to Cavendish's convincing account, Oldfield was another victim of the MI5 smearmongers, who, resentful of his appointment as supremo of Northern Ireland Intelligence and especially his pro-Catholic sympathies, put it about that he was a rabid homosexual. Oldfield was sacked and shortly afterwards died.

Mrs Thatcher and her supporters were all very outraged when Ken Livingstone recently attacked the late Airey

Neave for being involved with the MI5 campaign. Yet Mrs Thatcher made no effort at all to defend Oldfield against the smears when they were first published by Chapman Pincher. What makes it odder was that she obviously liked and admired him very much. Perhaps Mr Cavendish should now write a new book explaining the mystery.

My decision to write this book was not based on a desire to make money, but because I wished to defend the badly smeared reputation of a close friend and loyal Government servant when no effort to do so was made by the Government.

I first met the late Sir Maurice Oldfield – Chief of the Secret Intelligence Service and later Security Supremo in Ulster – in Cairo in 1946 when we were both intelligence officers in the Army, working for the Middle East office of MI5. He was a colonel and I was a lieutenant. We remained close friends until he died in 1981.

Few people are as close to each other as Oldfield and I were. We worked together, and spent much of our free time together. He knew my girlfriends and was best man both when I married Odile, my French wife, and later when I married Elspeth. Had he lived, he would have been a godfather to my son Julius. I stayed with Maurice's parents and know his brothers and sisters. He and I travelled in many countries together and had many mutual friends.

Maurice told me he had had some homosexual adventures in his student days, but the idea that he was a practising homosexual, when I knew him during thirty-five years, was absurd. However, with the introduction of positive vetting, intensified after the Kim Philby saga, serving SIS officers were asked various questions relating to their private lives, which touched on sex, gambling, political leanings, friendships, and so on. Maurice did not reveal that he had had some homosexual experiences when he was young.

Neither, incidentally, did most of the other numerous and active homosexuals in MI6.

I learned shortly after his death that a book was being written about him. I was told that there had been reports stating that he was a practising homosexual. I knew this allegation to be completely untrue and felt that I was duty-bound to defend my

xii

old friend's reputation. One way of doing this would have been to write a letter to *The Times*, but I decided more was required. I began to write a book, in which (I see from the index) there would be thirty pages which mention Oldfield.

I told the appropriate Government department – the Secret Intelligence Service or MI6 – that I was writing this book, and agreed to submit it to them when it was finished.

Subsequently, the book was abandoned, and I assumed pressure not to publish had been successfully applied. So I stopped work on my book, although my wife Elspeth wanted it finished so that my children would know something of my early life. In any event, the idea of a book was not popular with the Chief of MI6, Oldfield's successor.

Over Easter 1987, the smear campaign against Oldfield, which had been started in Ulster by 'Orange' elements, appeared as a banner headline and front-page story in a Sunday newspaper. To my mind, an immediate defence of Oldfield was now called for, which I undertook in collaboration with various newspapers and some excellent investigative reporting by Channel 4. We were able to destroy many details which were given to support the monstrous claims made about Oldfield.

But I decided that there remained a need for my book and quickly finished it. I then submitted it to the appropriate authorities – MI6. They said quite categorically, 'You cannot publish this.'

I gave thought to this before deciding that my loyalty to Maurice outweighed what I considered to be the unreasonable decision of a faceless civil servant.

I therefore had five hundred copies of my book printed, and I circulated them: mostly to people who had known Maurice, and to others in authority, such as members of both Houses of Parliament, judges, prominent civil servants, and so on – the Establishment, in other words. The *Sunday Times* broke the story of my 'Christmas card' just after Christmas 1987, and on 1 January 1988, the Government obtained an injunction against the *Observer* from publishing anything from this book.

Meanwhile, on 27 December 1987, I received a letter – delivered by motorcycle courier – from the Treasury Solicitor which, since it was marked 'Personal and Confidential', I cannot quote in full. It reminded me of the obligation of confidence 'to which it is considered you are subject'. It asked my intentions regarding the book, for a list of recipients, and said, 'The Government is considering its position.' My solicitor, Michael Lloyd, replied advising that my intentions were not formulated and that a list of recipients was not available. He said he would endeavour to reconstruct the list, if I so instructed him. When the Treasury Solicitor chased us, my solicitor replied to him saying I would seek to reconstruct the list when my secretary returned from holiday, but only 'as a courtesy'.

The Treasury Solicitor then asked for an undertaking that I would not distribute further copies without giving him fourteen days' notice. This I did; and on 1 March 1989, I gave notice that I was withdrawing this undertaking. Subsequent letters from the Treasury Solicitor warned I would be in contempt of court if I published further. There the matter has rested.

The literary journal *Granta* reproduced those parts of the book to which the Government took no exception. A copy of my manuscript was sent to the American magazine *Harpers*, who published what the Government had decreed was banned. The Government promptly announced that any copies shipped to the UK would be seized.

It is worth recalling that it was the earlier book, *Spycatcher*, published in the summer of 1987, which started the whole uproar, and led to the Government's continued (and perhaps ill-advised) fight against such publications, even though they had admitted in court that there was no breach of security in my book.

It was, of course, Peter Wright, a former MI5 officer who produced the book in order to make money because he claimed he had not been paid a proper pension. I reviewed *Spycatcher* in the *Guardian* (24 July 1987):

> *Spycatcher* is a very interesting book, first because of all the brouhaha regarding its publication and secondly because it is a very good read.
>
> But it raises a large number of serious questions for those interested in the workings of intelligence services,

whether they support the policy the Government has been pursuing, or the policy of 'publish and be damned' of certain newspapers.

Let me say at the beginning that as a former professional intelligence officer, I am shocked at the detail revealed by Peter Wright's memoirs, but more of that later. The point the Government has been trying to make in various courts is not what Wright reveals, but that he reveals it at all. The 'obligation of confidentiality' is the crux of the matter.

Sir Robert Armstrong claimed in court in Australia that some of Wright's revelations were dangerous to security. But he also claimed that Wright was in breach of his contract to keep his intelligence work confidential. I served in the Security Service (MI5) and the Secret Intelligence Service (MI6). When I left in 1953 I did not sign any form of declaration relating to confidentiality. I think this was for the simple reason that no such prepared document existed.

Such a document was produced, and all officers leaving the Service were required to sign it, after the Philby debacle. This document headed 'confidential' was called 'Supplementary Declaration on Termination of Engagement'.

In it the leaving officer accepts that the Head of the Service has *carte blanche* to cancel any entitlement the officer may have to superannuation or other benefits.

I believe Wright would have signed such a document because it was policy to do so when he left, and also since he was in receipt of a pension this would have been the basis of an ongoing and continuing contract. It is important to consider why Mr Wright should have written his book.

He complains his pension was small – and it was if the figure he gives of £2000 per annum is correct. He says he wanted to reveal the wrongdoing in MI5. To me this reads as the sprat to hook a publisher. The only important point is if part of the Government's security agency actually worked against the Prime Minister of the day.

Wright himself is an unusual character, whether as first seen in his TV documentary, or as the old man in the

Australian hat during the hearings in Melbourne, or from what one gleans about him from his book. From the cover of the book one would tend to believe Wright was a very important officer in MI5. 'A key figure' – 'The central figure in Britain's relentless and sometimes humiliating efforts to detect and expose Soviet espionage' – 'Britain's principal liaison with American intelligence officials' are some of the descriptions his publishers give him.

The uninformed could assume from some of the descriptions bandied about that Wright might have been the Number Two in MI5. Far from it. Neither of the intelligence services, MI5 or MI6, has a cadre of ranks like the services. Indeed, a recent head of an MI6 office abroad was so anxious not to be overlooked that he put in his *Who's Who* entry that his position carried the equivalent rank of Major General.

The British intelligence services divide primarily into junior and senior officers, with heads of department above them becoming directors, and above them the Head of the Service and his deputy. The breakdowns in the different levels of junior and senior officers relate primarily to salary, and not to the position or function the officer has.

It is said that when he joined MI5 Wright was told that he would be a senior officer, but also that he would never be eligible for a promotion. This seems an odd basis on which to start a career which after more than twenty years' service only merits a £2000 a year pension. Either Wright has magnified his importance or there must be something in the nod and the wink he said he was given about extra *ad hoc* payments.

Victor Rothschild's involvement in the Wright allegations intrigues me. When Maurice Oldfield decided to confess to lying in his positive vetting, he told me he discussed it with only three people: Sir Robert Armstrong, Victor Rothschild and myself. For six years Maurice's secret lay fallow until Chapman Pincher revealed it earlier this year. Who was Pincher's source? Wright and Pincher were brought together by Rothschild. Was the revelation about Oldfield timed to take the heat off the Wright case?

It may be useful, however, to consider the present position of the Secret Service officer who wants to write a book. The convention before Wright was that manuscripts concerning activities in the intelligence services would be submitted to the Service concerned. Sometimes they were acknowledged with a note: 'You would not expect us to comment.' On other occasions there was no acknowledgement and publication went ahead.

In 1965 I handed Oldfield a novel I had written about the collaboration of the KGB and MI6 in preventing the Chinese obtaining a nuclear device. Oldfield asked me to drop it and I did, but it could have been a very successful novel.

In 1985 a former SIS officer published a book about his experiences in Greece. When I brought this up in discussion with MI6, I was told, 'It slipped through.'

On 16 September 1985, I wrote to my former employers, MI6, advising I intended to write a book 'to protect Maurice'. For I knew then there was a book in the works to smear Maurice Oldfield's reputation. I sent with this letter a synopsis of my book. On 4 December 1986, I submitted to MI6 with an accompanying letter, 'the chapters of my book relating to my service in MI6'. I asked for written comments by 15 December. To date I have heard nothing more than demands from the Treasury Solicitor that I undertake not to publish.

Having read Wright's book I am not surprised at the row that erupted. It describes matters which have always been the most sensitive areas of intelligence. I find the detail that appears in *Spycatcher* shocking. It seems to me that the Government's case should have been to attack the revelation of confidential information and not to attack the contentious obligation of confidentiality. I realize that brings into question the recent flood of spy books, where retired officers have given information to authors.

Certainly new laws are required, for a secret service is

nothing if not secret. Meanwhile, my publishers and legal advisers seek to persuade the Treasury Solicitor that the Boy's Own Paper accounts of the adventures I went through thirty years ago, and which have been mentioned in other books, are harmless, and that the object of my book, which is to try and mitigate some of the damage done to the reputation of that loyal public servant, Sir Maurice Oldfield, can be accepted and permitted.

When an author writes a book to make money, it is hard not to believe that with his eye on maximum sales he will make his book controversial by revealing many things hitherto secret which will cause uproar. The main charge made by Wright was that a group of MI5 officers had contemplated treason in seeking to destabilize the Wilson Government.

Until *Spycatcher*, officers of the intelligence services (MI5, MI6 and GCHQ) submitted books they had written about their experiences to their former employers – who generally gave approval for publication, albeit with certain amendments, or returned the manuscript with a 'No comment' note which was, in effect, a green light.

In 1985, however, Nigel Clive, a former Secret Service officer, wrote a book called *A Greek Experience, 1943–1948* which he did not submit for approval but no action was taken against him. Clive has the good looks of a James Bond. A swashbuckling hero who parachuted into Greece in 1943, he joined MI6 on leaving the Army in 1945. He was posted to Jerusalem and then served in the Middle East, India, South-East Asia and Latin America.

His book reveals no secrets – any more than mine does – but on the basis of the Government's contention about the obligation of confidentiality as applied to former Secret Service officers, it should have been stopped.

As the *Spycatcher* case was fought through the courts in Australia, with the enormous amount of publicity which eventually turned it into a bestseller and made its author a millionaire, questions were asked in the House of Commons as to why the Government had not proceeded against me.

The Solicitor-General told MPs that there would be no further publication of my book without my giving him fourteen days' notice. The Government obtained injunctions to prevent publication because, they claimed, as a former member of the intelligence services I was bound to a lifelong duty of confidentiality. I denied this.

Although the Attorney General had said that the Government in no way contended that anything I had written breached security, its case in seeking injunctions was that no former Secret Service officer could write anything which in any way related to his time in the Secret Service.

The Government claimed that this lifelong duty of confidentiality was *ipso facto* part of the understood duty of intelligence officers. In my denial of this, I was supported by George Young, a former deputy chief of MI6, who told the *Guardian* that when he left the Service in 1963 the term 'obligation of confidentiality' was unknown. Richard Norton-Taylor of the *Guardian* contacted four former MI6 officers, who confirmed this to him. I was thus supported in my claim that when I left the Service in 1953, the term was unknown, and was an invention of this Government.

Mr Justice Kennedy, in the English court, told the Attorney General he would not ban the entire book and asked him to specify which parts were not contentious. As a result of Mr Justice Kennedy's judgment, two-thirds of the book were released from the ban in England. Thus, at one time, two-thirds of the book could be read in England and Wales but not a word of it in Scotland.

Obviously, there was great delight at the Law Lords' judgment, although I took strong exception to Lord Templeman, who, in his summing up, declared me 'disloyal'. I would have expected a former Gurkha officer to have some understanding for action in defence of a former comrade and colleague, as a matter of principle.

The whole crux of the issue, however, boils down to the Government's contention that Secret Service officers owe the Crown (whatever that is) a lifelong obligation of confidentiality. I was not formally advised of this either verbally or in writing – any more than I was asked when I joined the Service whether I was a Communist or a bugger. For that matter, neither was Kim Philby.

I know of two officers who withheld information regarding their earlier membership of the Communist Party, and I know that various members of the Secret Service, who had had homosexual experiences, withheld the fact when they were positively vetted. Today, I can remember half a dozen homosexuals who were members of the Service – and it was known what their tendencies were.

The Prime Minister's statement on 23 April 1987 could have done a lot more to defend a man who had virtually brought on the ill-health which killed him, by taking on the onerous duties of Intelligence Supremo in Northern Ireland. In her statement, Mrs Thatcher said:

> Sir Maurice Oldfield became Security Coordinator in Northern Ireland in October 1979. Subsequently, reports were received which caused his positive vetting clearance to be reviewed. In March 1980, in the course of that review, he made an admission that he had from time to time engaged in homosexual activities. His positive vetting clearance was withdrawn. By this time he was already a sick man; he finally ceased to serve as Security Coordinator in Northern Ireland when a successor took over in June 1980; he died in March 1981.
>
> There was a lengthy and thorough investigation by the Security Service, which included many interviews with Sir Maurice Oldfield himself, to examine whether there was any reason to suppose that he himself or the interests of the country might have been compromised.
>
> The conclusion was that, though his conduct had been a potential risk to security, there was no evidence or reason whatsoever to suggest that security had ever been compromised; indeed, he had contributed notably to a number of security and intelligence successes which would not have been achieved had there been a breach of security. That conclusion stands.

The draconian powers of the new Official Secrets Act (1988) have now come into force, although they seem to be being used more wisely.

Nobody with an intelligence background will think otherwise than that a Secret Service should be a secret, and it is right that the Government should take powers to safeguard the workings of the intelligence services.

However, where security is no longer at stake, it is pointless to deny potential authors the right to set down their experiences for the benefit of their families and friends and those interested in the intelligence world.

In an eloquent speech in parliament on 21 December 1988, on the subject of the Official Secrets Bill (1988), the Rt Hon. Julian Amery asked the Home Secretary not to close the door entirely on memoirs in the future.

Amery said, '. . . It is not unreasonable that, when [an intelligence officer] retires after a lifelong career – he may only have been in part-time service or loosely connected with it, as I have been – he would want to write something about it. So long as what he writes is not prejudicial to the safety of other members of the Service, the reputation of the Service or the national interest, he should be allowed to do so.'

It was the Minister of State at the Home Office, replying to Amery, who said, 'The sole criterion for authorizing publication is whether publication of a particular piece of information will jeopardize national security directly or indirectly. It is a judgement about considerations which are relevant today, not about past history or former embarrassments.'

Amery was as pleased as the rest of the retired intelligence community, who thought the hysteria which had beset the Government over *Spycatcher* was over.

However, in further debate in parliament on 13 February 1989, Jonathan Aitken drew attention to correspondence between Amery and the Home Secretary, in which the latter repudiated the undertaking given by the Minister of State.

Later in the debate on the same day, Amery spoke of his exhilaration and the satisfaction of hearing the Minister accept almost everything that he had advanced earlier. He was therefore greatly disturbed after the previous debate to receive a letter from the Home Secretary, which repudiated what he had earlier been told.

What the future holds for would-be ex-Secret Service authors is still not clear. After the Law Lords' decision, I wrote to my former employers and asked them whether they would reconsider their decision not to allow me to publish my book. I pointed out that anybody who wanted to read it had only to buy up seven or eight back copies of the *Scotsman*, or obtain the relevant copy of the American magazine *Harpers*.

In due course, I received a friendly reply advising that my book could not be 'authorized'. I had never asked that it be authorized, which I suppose amounted to getting the Government's seal of approval.

The former Chief Scientific Adviser to the Secret Intelligence Service, Professor R.V. Jones, published a book in November 1989 entitled *Reflections on Intelligence*, which, given the criteria exercised by the Government over *Inside Intelligence*, should also have been banned. However, there has been no public indication of the Government's displeasure at its appearance, and indeed, as a reviewer, I have read it carefully and found nothing in it to which anybody could object on a security basis.

A great deal of trouble was caused by my book, not because of a desire to cock a snook at my former employers, but because I wanted to show my support for Oldfield, my old friend and colleague. Friends in the media have helped enormously to undo some of the damage done to Oldfield's memory, and if, in the long run, all the legal wrangles result in Whitehall being more relaxed in its release of information, everything will not have been in vain.

There were obvious attempts to make me abandon the whole idea of the book, not only by the overt pressures of the Treasury Solicitor but by unfriendly remarks from people who failed to understand the principle which I was defending, and which should always be upheld. How else can families have some redress when a close relative is libelled? They have no defence.

That there were covert forces working against me became clear when, one after another, three newspapers known to support the Government started pestering me about my early life and my parents. It was suggested that I was born in Bulgaria, that my mother was a chambermaid and that my body was covered in scars so that I could only enter a swimming pool wearing a T-shirt.

My solicitor and I sought to kill these lies and distortions, and eventually we were told by the deputy editor of one of the newspapers that the perpetrator of these untruths was MI5.

On the other hand, I received support for what I was doing, not only from former colleagues in MI6, but from senior officers in the Armed Forces, as well as from Admiral Klose, Captain of the S208 and later Commander-in-Chief of the postwar German Navy, and from senior members of the police and judiciary.

They agreed that Maurice had had a raw deal and felt his defence was laudable.

I made contact with President Bush, a former Head of the Central Intelligence Agency, who sent a sympathetic letter wishing me 'good luck'.

But nobody could have supported me more than both Maurice's and my former boss, George Young.

This book is published for two good reasons: to maintain my support for a true friend, a true patriot; and for my children, who never knew Maurice but know today he was a true friend to us all.

The key dates in the saga of *Inside Intelligence* are as follows:

1 January 1988	Interim injunction prohibiting the *Observer* from publishing Cavendish memoirs.
2 January 1988	The *Observer* and *Sunday Times* obtain permission in the High Court to carry non-security-related extracts.
5 January 1988	The *Scotsman* carries details from the book. The Government obtains an interim interdict to stop further publication.
7 January 1988	The *Glasgow Herald* publishes more information.
12 January 1988	Lord Coulsfield, the judge who granted the interdict, changes his mind.
15 January 1988	English newspapers given permission to reproduce extracts not containing information Cavendish obtained while in security service.
18 January 1988	Following guidance from the Lord Advocate in the light of the English ruling, the *Scotsman* publishes more information.
26 January 1988	The *Scotsman*, *Herald* and STV appeal against interdict of 5 January.
29 January 1988	The Crown case collapses. The Lord Advocate applies for a fresh interdict and the media accept a voluntary ban.
16 February 1988	New hearing begins.
23 February 1988	Crown loses but appeals.
8 April 1988	Crown loses appeal in Court of Session, but appeals to House of Lords.
15–17 May 1989	Law Lords hear appeal.
6 July 1989	Law Lords reject appeal.

IN THE BEGINNING

In the bitter cold of the Russian winter, in a small village some hundreds of kilometres east of Moscow, during a howling gale and with darkness falling, a Russian peasant is wandering home to his meagre village. Suddenly he stops as he sees a small game bird on the ground, nearly dead from cold and privation. The peasant picks up the bird and warms it. The bird soon recovers and the peasant wonders what to do next. At that moment a herd of cattle come by and one of them drops a large dollop right in front of him. Realizing that if he puts the bird in the steaming cow's dollop, the bird will stay warm until morning and then be able to fly away, he does this and then goes home. But a second peasant comes along after the first one has gone and hears the bird chirping happily to itself in the steaming mess. This peasant seizes the bird, breaks its neck and takes it home for supper.

This old intelligence story has three morals:

1 Do not believe that everybody who drops you in the shit is your enemy.
2 Do not believe that everybody who gets you out of the shit is your friend.
3 Whenever you *are* in the shit keep quiet about it.

CHAPTER 1

THE PHILOSOPHY AND MORALITY of the career officer in the British Secret Service need to be examined fully to be understood.

The traitors exposed since the war have not been entirely from one social class. Philby (whom I counted as a drinking companion), McLean and Burgess dealt a death blow to the cherished but false concept that as long as the Foreign and Secret Services were run by gentlemen, security would take care of itself.

It is well known that Stewart Menzies, while Chief of MI6, spent a great deal of time recruiting officers and discussing intelligence matters in White's Club which, then as now, is the ultimate in London's clubland. At dinner one evening, one of my guests asked Julian Amery if it would be possible for Julian to help him join the Carlton. Julian replied by recounting the story of William Pitt who, when Prime Minister, was walking past White's with a friend.

Pitt's friend asked, 'Prime Minister, would it be possible for you to propose me for White's?'

To which Pitt reputedly replied, 'At the end of the year we shall be making some new viscounts and some new barons. Could you accept a viscountcy instead?'

The qualifications for intelligence have sometimes been as rarefied. Before the war a 'gentleman', in the sense of being suitable for trustworthy but secretive service to the Crown, would certainly have had to have had a respectable pedigree, public school education, and probably to have been an officer in one of the Services. Until the advent of communism and the collapse of imperial Europe, the intelligence services of our potential European enemies, particularly Germany, were staffed by people of similar background.

However, with the revolution of the proletariat, post-First World War intelligence operations by the Russians were carried out by people who despised the whole class system; and with a Labour government in power in Britain from 1945, recruitment to the highest and most confidential levels of secret government service was in for a drastic change.

There were, therefore, two areas of recruitment for communist intelligence services when targeting the West. The well-born before the last war were, in general, disgusted by the excesses of communist expansion and were, by instinct, fairly right-wing. The majority showed sympathy for fascism and opposed communism. There were some, however, who felt (as many young men going up to university do) that there was much good in socialism and communism. The vast majority were not so drawn that they could be turned to betray their country, and, as they grew older and more experienced, they realized that the philosophies were probably unworkable – human beings being what they are.

With the postwar entrant to government service from working- or lower middle-class circles, a new but different catchment area of potential Soviet agents became available.

I believe that working for a secret intelligence service almost always brings about a state of mind which permits anything if it is done for the benefit of the service and hence for the good of one's country.

Let us consider an example. Almost any Soviet official is worth recruiting as a conscious or an unconscious agent. Let us suppose that a diplomat working in the Soviet Embassy in Warsaw is known to have indulged in the black market or to have had an extramarital affair with a non-Soviet woman, or indeed to have had a homosexual affair during his posting. Should any of this come to the notice of a Western intelligence service, then the Soviet diplomat has laid himself open to being blackmailed into working against his own country. He must decide whether he wishes to face punishment and the probable end to his promising career, or make a different choice; for, apart from being open to black-mail, he is also told that if he succumbs to this blackmail the Western agency involved will pay money into a Swiss bank account for him, and, in due course, will arrange his escape from the East and see that he is resettled safely and anonymously in the West.

By use of blackmail a Soviet source may be recruited directly, in which case he is a conscious agent.

A Russian may also be recruited indirectly. Let us suppose that either the lover, male or female, or the black market contact of the Soviet official we are considering is the one contacted by the Western agency. This intermediary may be forced by threat of blackmail to obtain information from the Soviet official, either during bedroom activities or while sharing black market spoils. In this case the Russian official is unconsciously supplying information to an agent who has succumbed to blackmail.

Blackmail can be used either to recruit a conscious source or to recruit an agent who will run an unconscious source.

Blackmail can be used in other ways, for example, by threats to the family of valuable informants. An operative member of MI6 cannot automatically rule out such methods of achieving the required result in an intelligence mission. Similarly, theft, deception, lies, mutilation and even murder are considered if and when necessary.

An SIS officer lies from his first day in the Service. It is part of his cover. He says he is a member of the Foreign Service, or he works at the Ministry of Defence, or he is involved in Post Office engineering, or whatever else his cover might be. As the years go by, the lies take over from the truth and morality accepts the other demands which are made on an officer to get the job done.

In assessing sources of information, various essential questions have to be asked. Perhaps the most important is motive. Why is the agent passing this information to a foreign intelligence service? Rarely is the source an idealist who feels he or she is helping to put the world to rights. (Penkowsky was one such agent.) The trouble with an idealistic agent is that he may exaggerate a situation, seeking to influence the course of action taken by the recipient of his information. Great reliance, therefore, must be placed on the case officer, who must judge whether the source is slanting information for his own idealistic ends. Naturally, original documents or copies of documents are invaluable.

We then come to the mercenary agent, one who is passing

information in return for regular payments or some other material benefit. Provided the information is substantiated by documentary evidence, this is the most common and probably the most satisfactory agent to handle. The case officer knows where he stands with his source. It is true that the source may seek to get extra payment by doctoring information to make it look more important, but provided the relationship between source and case officer (or source through head agent to case officer) is satisfactory, this is the arrangement by which most services operate. A further advantage is that the source plays into the hands of the Service by signing receipts for funds received, and consequently lays himself open to blackmail when he eventually becomes reluctant to continue working.

Then there is the agent who is set up for blackmail from the beginning. The groundwork having been laid and the agent having been photographed in bed with a small boy or his boss's wife, he is then forced to provide information. The relationship between this source and his case officer will, obviously, never be as friendly or trustworthy as it would have been in other circumstances.

If the arrangement under which the source provides intelligence to his case officer is satisfactory, the next most important consideration is the access open to that agent. It would be ridiculous for a high-level functionary in the Ministry of Foreign Trade in Moscow to produce minutes of Politburo meetings, because there would be no reason for them to come into his possession. On the other hand, a secretary who took minutes or a clerk who made copies of such minutes and worked in the Politburo secretariat would have natural access to such information.

The foregoing raises a few considerations about the morality of those who obtain information by methods commonly used by intelligence services. All too often an agent is caught by the opposing service, and that service immediately seeks to obtain as much information as possible from the captured agent.

In the first twenty years of the Cold War, physical torture and brutality were commonplace. Since few agents once captured were able to withstand the refined methods of the KGB, which included use of heat, cold, electric shock, lack of sleep, starvation and treatment intended to bring on disorientation, MI6 agents who were in a position to be caught were issued with an L (lethal) tablet. These were concealed either in a hollow tooth or in a ring and when swallowed resulted in instantaneous death.

I remember particularly well one occasion when Maurice Oldfield was called upon as Chief to authorize whether or not an L tablet should be smuggled in to a source who, if he broke under interrogation, would bring about the deaths of several other SIS agents with whom he had been working. Despite his strong religious convictions, Maurice took the only course he could.

Things have changed in recent years. The unmasking of traitors (if they are against us) or agents (if they are working for us) has been done mainly by defectors. Nobody can be precise about the number of Western agents who were rounded up as a result of George Blake's treason and subsequent escape, just as the revelation that Blake had betrayed his colleagues in SIS came to us from a defector. But it was not always so.

CHAPTER 2

'OF COURSE YOU'LL BE SAFE,' I promised the young girl. 'Nothing can happen.'

I was twenty-three and she was a few years younger. We could have been lovers but there was more to it than that: she was one of our agents and I had been her first contact in the West. Now I was sending her back.

This episode had begun almost a year before in the summer of 1950, when Big John, the local Chief for MI6, called me to his office, in a small anonymous spa town in Western Germany which housed the biggest operational headquarters of MI6 in Europe.

The Cold War was then at its height and we lived with an ever-present threat that the Red Army could overrun us within forty-eight hours if the rumours of war became a reality. We had our agents scattered through the garrison towns of East Germany to give us early warning of any troop build-up. And we had our agents at the main rail centres, like Frankfurt on Oder, where the movement of flat rail cars was recorded for us.

At the various crossing points from Russia into Poland, and from Poland into East Germany, our agents equipped with cumbersome W/T sets reported back the numbers of Soviet military vehicles and the numbers painted on tanks, so that our order of battle for the Red Army could constantly be updated and studied.

John offered me a chair, waited until I was sitting down, then mentioned that he had an interesting job for me.

I was often given the *ad hoc* assignments. Probably because I was the youngest officer in the Service; perhaps also because I had a background in R5 training – that section of MI6 Headquarters in London responsible for studying the Russian intelligence services and organizing counterespionage, founded by Kim Philby.

If the Red Army did overrun Western Germany, then an evacuation plan already existed for the British Army and its camp followers, and for the Control Commission for Germany and its families. But John felt that MI6 could not afford to rely on a general evacuation scheme.

'Reconnoitre the coast, Tony,' he said, 'and find me a suitable port in Holland or Germany from which we can handle a Dunkirk operation.'

I always enjoyed handling jobs which sent me off on my own. So it was with relief I packed a bag and threw it into the back of a small black Volkswagen Beetle, the car with which most of us were equipped.

Our unit also had its fleet of black Humber Super Snipes which, while comfortable, fast and fairly reliable, attracted enormous attention. As they were the only black Humbers then in Germany, the whisper 'Secret Service' followed them wherever they sped.

The afternoon was hot and still, with only a few birds singing, as I headed out of our small spa towards Minden and then followed the slow course of the river Weser as it ran north through farmland towards the bay of Heligoland – Minden, Wienberg followed.

With the day already dying, I drove towards Wittmund, looking for a pub or *Gasthaus* in which to spend the night.

Early next morning I drove to the sea at Nordeich, and, as I began to memorize the coast, I passed two bronzed young hitch-hikers. A man and a young woman, both strikingly fair, dressed in tight lederhosen, still typical then of German youth.

I stopped, reversed and let them aboard.

'Hello,' I said, 'I'm Paul.'

They told me they were brother and sister and were from Prenzlau, on the way to Stettin.

At this I pricked up my ears. Prenzlau was an important Soviet base, where we didn't have an agent but could definitely use one. From then on my interest in this pair was professional, and I started to consider how to recruit them for intelligence.

They were camping rough and were enjoying the freedom and late summer sunshine of the West German countryside. My cover during this period was as a Control Officer, a low-grade civil servant working for the Control Commission which administered the British zone of recently conquered Germany. With our access to the NAAFI, where duty-free cigarettes, chocolate, coffee and alcohol were available, we were all fabulously rich by German standards. On the black market a small tin of Nescafé was equivalent to a man's weekly pay packet, and most girls would still do almost anything for some instant chocolate or coffee.

I invited my new friends to have a meal and after much ravenous eating and drinking they booked a room between them in the inn at which I had already decided to spend the night.

We talked late into the early morning about the complexity of politics, about the Russians and about the tragedy of divided Germanies. And as I half suspected, they were not brother and sister but lovers.

The girl's name was Frieda, the boy's was Alfred. They always knew me as Paul. Frieda and Alfred had another ten days before they were due back at their studies – he as an architect, she as a student biologist.

I quickly discovered that they were intensely anti-Russian, having seen their city occupied, and explained that they could be of great use to the West.

After a further day's talking – and food – we finally agreed that Alfred would spend the next week on his own, comforted by funds from me courtesy of His Majesty's Government, while I would take Frieda to be trained as our agent in Prenzlau. Before doing this, I telephoned my office in Bad Salberg and had Alfred and Frieda traced through our records and registry. Back came the go-ahead to recruit Frieda. Alfred and I decided that the three of us would meet up again in West Berlin a week later. Alfred was immediately to cross back into East Germany on foot, the way they both had come, while I flew Frieda up to Berlin on an RAF transport plane and installed her and me in our safe flat in Ploener Strasse, in the Grunewald district of West Berlin.

There Frieda was trained as a W/T (wireless telegraphy) operator and was taught cyphers using a one-time code pad. She met her case officer, a member of the Berlin station of ISRU (which was in fact called something entirely different). He, not me, would from now on direct her activities and meet her whenever she came to Berlin. He would send a courier to her whenever she needed funds, a spare part for her set, or courage.

Frieda's training completed, we met up again with Alfred, and then the two of them set off back to their homes in Prenzlau.

On their arrival, advised by a coded telephone call to a safe telephone number in East Berlin giving news of a sick aunt, we sent in a courier with Frieda's radio. Three weeks later – on schedule – Frieda came up on the air and we had another active agent *in situ* at an important Soviet base. It was some six months later that Frieda came to Berlin, and her case officer contacted me to say that she wanted to see me urgently.

I met her and took her to dinner in a quiet restaurant near the Berlin Zoo. She was as beautiful as ever but unhappy, and told me that her relationship with Alfred was no longer so close. Alfred, it seemed, suspected her of having had an affair with me while she had been training.

Although this was untrue, it quickly became obvious to us both that we were heading in that direction. The price, it seemed, of her returning to Prenzlau was for me to replace Alfred in her affections.

I warned Frieda that this could lead to difficulties, even to Alfred's jealousy leading him to denounce her. But it was what she wanted.

Frieda's work had become very important for us, and, much as I disliked it, I had to send her back. So it was with promises of passion and future happiness that I saw the girl on to the U-bahn that headed east.

I saw Frieda again once more after that, two months later. She told me then that she thought she was being watched, but that Alfred still seemed friendly and that she trusted him. She had promised him that she had severed her connections both with me and her case officer. Nevertheless, she did not want to return to Prenzlau but begged to be allowed to stay in the West.

It took a lot of persuasion to get her to go back. I never saw her again. Shortly afterwards she was caught, tried and shot. She was nineteen. I was twenty-three. When I reflect now on how ruthless I was at twenty-three, I see how different the world, its circumstances and its people are today. Let me try and explain how my experiences have shaped my world.

CHAPTER 3

MY CLEAREST MEMORY FROM before the last war is of riding down the slopes into the small mountain village of Pontresina on Saturday, 2 September 1939, and hearing Swiss peasants shouting '*Es git krieg*', the Swiss-German rendering of 'It gives war'. And so it did.

I was perched atop an old wooden cart, laden with hay, which one of the farmers of the village was bringing down from the Bernina region to store in his barn as winter fodder.

The cart was being pulled by a Swiss cow called Rosa. The old peasant, known as Neeni, would direct the cow by blows on either side of her nose and if he wanted her to speed up he would whack her casually across the rump.

As for countless millions of others, the war was to have a great effect on my life. My mother had first taken me to Switzerland as a small boy in 1932. After the loss of my father she decided to spend most of her time in Switzerland, a country whose mountains she loved dearly and where she thought I might receive a useful education. The last was true.

By the time I was fourteen, I spoke English, German, Swiss-German and French equally well, and in the presence of foreigners in Switzerland I was invariably accepted by them as a young Swiss peasant.

Being accepted by the Swiss boys themselves was less easy.

Two experiences from those elementary school days are lodged in my memory.

One summer's afternoon – I was about eight – we were playing Red Indians. We were all Indians, for the Swiss did not believe in cowboys! I had been captured and was due to be tortured. It was all in fun, but this time the fun had a serious ending.

One of my young captors had a bright idea. Tie him to the telegraph pole near the wasps' nest. A good torture for '*der Englander*'.

It was. They shook the nest and I was stung over one hundred times, and nearly died.

The other incident which sticks in my memory was when I was hurled into a gargantuan pile of manure. Most visitors to Switzerland in the autumn will have seen those vast piles of cow manure in the corners of meadows which grow, grow and grow during the winter months while the cattle are indoors, and which are used in the autumn to spread over the fields to fertilize the ground as the snow melts. During the summer the *Mist*, as the Swiss call it, forms a thick crust on the surface. One happy day my Swiss friends grabbed me and threw me into it for no particular reason. I plunged through the crust and into the sticky morass below. I might easily have drowned or choked – but fortunately was pulled out by a grinning farmworker.

We were a tough crowd, and by the time I was ten I could walk up the back of Diavolezza, a famous ski run where there is an uphill climb of about three hours and a run down of over ten kilometres over the Morteratsch Glacier. This we could do twice in a day.

The coming of the war, however, stopped my chances of going on to a school in French Switzerland and my mother decided that, in a time of war, she preferred to be in her own country. We came back to England by train in April 1940, a journey which took somewhat longer than it should have done because our train did not have the priority of a troop train. As there was then no through train to the Channel, we changed in Paris and crossed over to the Gare du Nord and travelled on to Calais.

It was as we were boarding the steamer that the port was attacked. All I remember is crouching on the floor of the cabin, listening to the bombs, alternating between being afraid and trying to comfort my mother. We crossed the Channel safely that night and arrived back in England, where I continued growing up like any other boy during the war.

In due course, when the chance arose, I volunteered for the Army. Contrary to the general belief that the Army invariably sticks round pegs in square holes, the powers that be decided I had a certain linguistic ability. After some initial infantry training which consisted mainly of running up and down wet mountains in North Wales (one of my fellow recruits, later to become a sergeant-major in the Intelligence Corps, was Bryan Forbes, now a bestselling thriller writer and film director). I was sent to the School of Oriental and African Studies in London to learn Japanese.

There we were taught the language by a tall bearded gentleman called Professor Daniels, and by a beautiful young woman of film star appearance and proportions called Carmen, as well as by a group of Canadian *nisai* (Canadian citizens of at least three generations pure Japanese descent) in uniform with the rank of sergeant-major or warrant-officer.

The students at the school were from all three Services and of all ranks from private up to captain, or its equivalent in the Air Force or Navy. Our studies took place in Sussex Square, just behind Lancaster Gate tube station, where a sentry kept watch in front of our building with its sign SAULT (Services Administrative Unit for Language Training) which 'announced' to passers-by what went on. It was the first of many times that my job was hidden by a fairly anonymous collection of letters, which seems to be a speciality of the British intelligence community. At this time my mother was living in London in Campden Hill, and was thus within walking distance of my classes. And so I was given permission to live out, and given a living-out allowance which increased my total income to something like £7 a week.

Early in 1945 I was twice whisked away from the school to assist in interrogating captured Germans, once with the 43rd (Wessex) Division and once just outside Brussels with a counter-intelligence unit.

After VE day the pace of our study speeded up at a time when most of us had begun to slow down. When the war was in Europe and on our doorstep we had felt involved, but now that the only fighting was almost ten thousand miles away, a certain laxity affected us.

For my part, I decided that neither the Japanese nor the Far East interested me and asked to be returned to my unit. This was not a popular move, but on the other hand I was certainly not one of their best students. I was therefore posted to the Intelligence Corps Depot which was in Wentworth Woodhouse, the home of the Earl of Northesk, just outside Sheffield. The question of my Army career then had to be considered.

To be commissioned in the Intelligence Corps for anybody under twenty-five was at this time unheard of, and the most likely direction my military service would have taken was for me to become a corporal in some Field Security Unit.

However, Army orders (or perhaps it was King's regulations) laid down that any soldier who wished to be considered for a commission should be allowed to go before a Wosby (War Office Selection Board). With the speedy development of the Far East War the need was for cannon fodder in the Far East; in other words, infantry officers. A further alternative was to apply for parachute training.

To be doubly sure I applied for both. And in due course my Company Commander, a very red-faced, hard-drinking major in the Royal Scots Fusiliers, allowed me and two others to travel south from Wentworth for a weekend in a country house, where we were monitored in various ways to see if we were suitable to be officers and gentlemen.

Gathered together were about thirty aspiring candidates and we were set a series of tests designed to show that we could think clearly, were not utterly cowardly, had some pretension of leadership and were educated beyond the standard of a fourteen-year-old schoolboy.

We also attended various interviews. As I recall, I was the only candidate who had to see both the psychiatrist and the psychologist. The latter was a cheery soul who told me afterwards that I was a sentimental cynic.

In later years I have come to see that he was very perceptive.

Bored by the whole thing, the three of us who had come down from Wentworth felt that no one would be any the wiser if we took a day off in London on the way back to our unit, and this we did. On arriving back in camp twenty-four hours later we were surprised to find that our absence had been immediately noticed and we were all put on charges of being absent without leave.

The next morning we were marched in front of 'Blue Nose',

the gentleman with the red face, who told us loudly and at length that any chance we had of becoming officers would go down the drain if he sentenced us to a term of arrest. As we had carried back with us in sealed envelopes an indication of our performance at the Wosby, he already knew that two out of the three of us had been selected for officer training; and so after a severe lecture about irresponsibility not being the way to a commission, he dismissed us.

In due course orders came for me to report to the Pre-Octu (Officer Cadet Training Unit) at Wrotham in Kent. As the date was still seven weeks off and my application for a parachute course had also come through, I was able to do that before going on to Wrotham, where I duly arrived entitled to an extra three-pence a day as a parachutist.

I cannot remember now how it came about, or who suggested it, but during my first days at Wrotham I was summoned to the War Office for a further interview, as a result of which it was decided that I should be commissioned as an intelligence officer. At the end of the six weeks at Wrotham I moved to the Basic Octu at Mons Barracks in Aldershot.

The course there took a further six weeks and two things still stand out in my memory. The first was the regimental sergeant-major, the immortal 'Tubby' Brittan; over six foot tall, twenty-two stone, and bulging out everywhere under the blue and white cap of the Coldstream Guards. The other thing I remember, still with great surprise, is that I won the Octu five-mile walk.

At the end of the course and after a boisterous party in the Queens Hotel at Farnborough, I was commissioned into the Intelligence Corps at nineteen, sent briefly on leave, and then posted to Cairo where, on arrival in an intelligence job, I immediately put up a second pip and became a full lieutenant intelligence officer. From then on I was always several years younger than my colleagues.

CHAPTER 4

IT WAS IN CAIRO that I first met Maurice Oldfield, then my boss but later Chief of MI6 and a friend.

It was June 1946 and one of the first big differences in my commissioned life was the travelling. From being one of eight or more other ranks booked into a third-class compartment, I now sat in comfort in first class with a maximum of three to a side.

I journeyed down to Dover and took the ferry to Boulogne. There I moved into a pleasant transit camp on the Channel beaches and, after two days, boarded what had once been the Blue Train, the luxurious express to the Riviera. Forty-eight hours later I arrived on the Riviera at Hyères, where again I was accommodated in a tented transit camp. I spent over a week here, going off to Le Lavandou daily to lie on the beach and eye wistfully the local female population. I would happily have stayed there all the summer, but instead the machinery of military management clicked into gear and I was ushered on to a troop ship, the *Donnatter Castle*, and after a pleasant but hot cruise found myself in a dusty tented transit camp in Port Said. A very slow train then took me to Cairo and Almaza transit camp.

Two days later I reported in to a major in GSI(X), the manpower section of General Staff Intelligence, and he sent me for an impossibly casual interview with an aged captain in SIME (Security Intelligence Middle East). I appear to have had what the aged captain was looking for. A day later I returned for a further interview with a young lieutenant colonel, Maurice Oldfield, who was to have a great influence on my life for the next thirty-five years: 'the formidable Maurice Oldfield', as Kim Philby called him.

When I was shown into Maurice's office I saw a plump and

15

owl-faced lieutenant colonel with untidy hair, wearing spectacles and dressed in rumpled khaki drill bush shirt and shorts, with one sock dangerously lower than the other.

At that stage in my youthful military career I was not used to dealing with colonels, but I remember being somewhat surprised when this particular colonel stood up to shake hands with me; which I thought was both kind and polite, though odd. He then asked me to sit down. We talked about what I had done and, since I was nineteen, there was not a great deal to tell. The only interesting and unusual part of my life was that I had been educated in Switzerland, and was something of a linguist. We talked about this, and the war generally, and touched briefly on the problems facing the British in Palestine.

I did not know at that time that SIME was the Middle East office of MI5 and Maurice did not enlighten me. What he did tell me at the end of the interview, which lasted about thirty minutes, was that I would be posted to SIME and that I would work for him. And he explained to me that all the officers in SIME, whether military or civilian, lived on the local economy and not in a military mess. He then summoned the admin. officer and told him to give me the necessary Army documentation and a car with a driver.

I went out to my barren transit camp, packed up my kit and moved into a reasonably comfortable flat in Zamalek, which I was to share with a fellow officer. That afternoon, driving out to Almaza in the car provided, I reflected that this was a very different kind of colonel and a very different kind of Army with which I was now involved.

Oldfield had approved me, and thus, a bare four weeks after I'd finished tramping around in hobnail boots on a parade ground, I became a two-pip lieutenant in the Middle East office of MI5, working in the Jewish terrorist section.

The Head of SIME was Brigadier Douglas Roberts, a magnificent soldier who had grown up in Russia, rather as I had in Switzerland, and consequently spoke beautiful and fluent Russian. He was responsible directly to MI5 in London but also administratively – as we were an Army unit – through the Chief of the General Staff to the Commander-in-Chief. Under Douglas Roberts SIME divided into two, with Oldfield in charge of what was called the

B Division and a quiet wing commander from the RAF in charge of A Division.

I knew little of what A Division did, but B Division's principal task at this time was dealing with the activities of the three illegal organizations operating in Palestine against the British: the Hagannah, the IZL[1] and the Stern Gang.

SIME was housed in an old apartment block just outside the barbed wired compound of Grey Pillars, known officially as General Headquarters Middle East Forces. While I was still part of it, it changed its name to Middle East Land Forces.

Among the many interesting and extrovert characters serving in GSI in Cairo then was Claude Dewhurst, who drove an enormous car known as 'Merki Bey'. *Bey* was an Egyptian title given to anybody of the seniority of colonel or higher, and, in some ways, was the equivalent of our lowest order of knighthood. The car was in fact a battered Mercedes 540K, and Dewhurst always had a *suffragi* (Egyptian servant) standing by with a bucket of water whenever he started the car. Flames belched forth from it like a Chinese New Year's dragon, and Claude's departure was watched and applauded each day. Occasionally, the spectators were treated to the sight of somebody or something catching fire.

Dewhurst later went on to be Military Attaché in Belgrade. When we met again in 1950 he was a brigadier and Head of the British Liaison Mission to the Soviet Commander-in-Chief, based in Berlin and Potsdam, while I was in Berlin as the MI6 War Planning Officer.

Dewhurst's boss was Brigadier Geoffrey MacNab, a distinguished Highland soldier who went on to become Military Attaché in Paris and later Secretary of the Government Hospitality Fund in London.

Cairo at that time was truly a Paris of the East, and to me at nineteen it was paradise. Perfect hot climate, a comfortable way of life, breathtaking women and an interesting job with allowances and pay of nearly £100 a month, which seemed a fortune.

I quickly acquired an old twin Triumph 350cc motorbike and was able to explore the surrounds of Cairo and, at weekends, run

---

[1] Irgun Zvai Leumi.

out to Alexandria, Port Said, Ismailia and Suez. But it was not all women and motorbikes.

SIME's tentacles stretched out through the whole of the friendly and not so friendly Middle East, with its own outstations in every country where British Armed Forces had a writ. Thus there were defence security officers as the chief MI5 representatives in all the countries from Libya up to Syria. In Baghdad there was a unit operating under RAF cover known as CICI;[1] SIME's influence was also felt within such organizations as CSDIC,[2] which operated the Interrogation Centre at Maadi, a suburb of Cairo, and with people like SOILEM (Staff Officer Intelligence Levant and Mediterranean) who operated out of Port Said and who at the time was a middle-aged Marine colonel.

There was also Air Intelligence and, of course, there was close liaison with the Secret Service, better known as MI6 and known to us in the Middle East at this time as ISLD, or the Inter Services Liaison Department. Each defence security officer had his own network running through assistant DSOs who, for example in Egypt, were located in Port Said and Ismailia and Suez, as well as Cairo. These men in turn controlled field security sections which also liaised with the SIB (Special Investigation Branch) of the Military Police.

As a young intelligence officer I became almost a law unto myself, certainly as far as military authorities were concerned, with the issue of a prized green security card. This carried my photograph and description in a three-fold green card printed in English and Arabic, and advised all and sundry that 'the bearer is engaged in security duties and is authorized to be *in any place at any time in any dress*', signed for and on behalf of the Commander-in-Chief by a colonel. The card also enjoined all people subject to the jurisdiction of the Commander-in-Chief to give me every assistance of which I might stand in need. It was invaluable!

No sooner had I arrived in SIME than terrorists blew up the King David Hotel in Jerusalem, killing ninety-one people and severely injuring many others. Of the dead, twenty-eight were

[1] Counter Intelligence Centre Iraq.
[2] Combined Services Detailed Interrogation Centre.

British and forty-one were Arabs, but also among those killed were seventeen Jews and five other Europeans.

There will always be controversy over whether this massacre was deliberate, since IZL claimed they telephoned warnings of the imminent explosion to newspapers and the police. Investigation afterwards showed that nobody had received any sort of warning before the explosion but that a newspaper office and a telephonist in the Government secretariat *had* received telephone calls relating to a bombing after the explosion had taken place.

It is claimed by the people involved that a message passed to the police and relayed by them to the Chief Secretary John Shaw gave warning before the explosion, but was contemptuously dismissed by Shaw, who said he was not in the habit of following instructions given by the Jews. Shaw himself denies this, there is no evidence to support it and the whole matter became the subject of a libel action in 1948, which Shaw won.

The King David Hotel contained not only military head-quarters and the High Commissioner's secretariat but also operated as a hotel and restaurant. It was difficult, therefore, to control access since the hotel was a smart place for the local populace to take tea. Early on the morning of 22 July the IZL stole a number of vehicles, including a small truck on to which they loaded milk churns stuffed with high explosives. This was then driven down to the basement service entrance of the hotel.

The terrorists were undetected, or at least unhindered, as they unloaded the deadly milk churns and placed them directly under the secretariat offices. The Jewish terrorists, dressed as Arabs, then escaped on foot towards their getaway vehicle, a stolen taxi. Just half an hour after midday and about an hour after the explosives had been placed, they detonated. All six floors of a corner of the King David Hotel collapsed, burying many of the dead and wounded in the rubble.

The atrocity of the King David thus had the opposite effect to that intended by the IZL. It stiffened the attitude of the military who were, to a large extent, pro-Arab and anti-semitic anyway.

The Army Commander at this time was Lieutenant General Evelyn Barker whose office was in the old city. He was very much the rugged soldier and he published an order blaming the general

Jewish public for their passive support of the terrorists, and added that he wanted them to be 'made aware of the contempt and loathing with which we regard them'. He also ordered the cessation of social intercourse between the British soldiers and the Jews.

After spending four weeks familiarizing myself with in-depth briefing about the background to Jewish terrorist activity, and meeting the Jewish Agency's Intelligence Liaison Officer in Cairo with whom we had a very good relationship, I flew up to Jerusalem in an RAF Dakota.

During those early days in Palestine I worked alongside many members of the Palestine police and found them to be a very tough but fiercely efficient organization. Among others serving there were Dick Catling (later Sir Richard), whom I was later to visit several times in Nairobi where he became Commissioner of the Kenya Police and did a magnificent job in dealing with the troubles there, and Ken Newman (later Sir Kenneth) whom I later visited in Belfast, at the Police College in Hampshire and in London where he was Commissioner of Police. It was Ken Newman who was Chief Constable of the RUC during the troubled times when Maurice Oldfield first became Security Supremo for Northern Ireland. Many of those who have worked with Sir Kenneth rate him as the finest policeman this country has yet produced.

The man to whom I was administratively responsible while in Palestine was the Defence Security Officer, Sir Gyles Isham, a lieutenant colonel in the KRRC, a baronet and a well-known pre-war Shakespearian actor. Isham left the Army before the pull-out of British forces and was succeeded by Bill Magan, an Indian Army officer who later became Head of SIME. Isham was one of those – myself included – who left the Army to join MI6 under Oldfield, and in due course our paths crossed again.

The character I am least of all likely to forget was Major A.L.S. Callan, known affectionately throughout the intelligence world as Abu Ali. Callan was a large, middle-aged man with a considerable girth and capacity for pleasure. He had worked in the Middle East with the oil companies for most of his life and was consequently a fine Arabist. There were times when his help and advice were of the greatest use in solving some of the problems I faced. After the British withdrawal from Palestine Major Callan moved down to Cairo and worked there with SIME. He often took me through narrow dangerous streets on tours of some of the houses of lesser repute and introduced me to the madams as his son. Thus I became known as Bin Abu Ali or the son of Abu Ali.

I was to have one sinister and unforgettable adventure in Palestine before Ernest Bevin made his decision to withdraw from Palestine, leaving a mess that could only continue into further violence.

I had been working undercover, disguised as an escaped German prisoner-of-war, when events overtook me. So I returned thankfully to my own nationality – but continued to use an assumed name.

I came up to Palestine from Kabrit in Egypt in July 1947 on a mission. I was riding in a jeep from Jerusalem to the Palestine Police School at Ramallah and then on to Haifa, with my driver. We were both armed with side-arms and I also kept a 9mm Beretta inside my jacket. Our jeep was waved down at a makeshift roadblock by what we took to be British soldiers, so we slowed down and stopped.

The four men who stopped us were dressed in British khaki uniforms and were wearing regulation steel helmets, but we soon realized that they were terrorist members of either the Stern Gang or the IZL. They dragged us swiftly from the jeep, which they then drove off the road into a wadi. My protest was answered by a blow in the face from a British rifle butt which rendered me almost unconscious. Fortunately, I wasn't wearing my Intelligence Corps badges but, in keeping with the authority given me in my green card, always wore whatever badges suited a particular job. On this occasion I was wearing the badges of the Royal Army Service Corps, as was my driver; and our jeep had a Service Corps blue and yellow square divided into two triangles, but it seemed that this was not about to save us.

'You. Where are you going? Which unit are you from?' Our captors were questioning me repeatedly but had not yet gone through my pockets where they would have found my green card and exposed us as part of the intelligence system.

After several more questions, punctuated by punches and blows from the rifle butt, the terrorists suddenly stopped questioning us and fled, leaving us stunned and bloody.

Relieved and grateful for large mercies, we clambered into the jeep and drove it back to the road. It turned out that the terrorists had wrongly identified the approach of three armoured cars on the dusty road as an anti-terrorist patrol. By now there was considerable traffic and it was almost breakfast time. We drove in silence to the Police School where we were able to wash, have our wounds treated and give an account of what had happened. We were soon to discover that both of us – the driver and I – had come too close to kidnapping and an ugly death.

What was behind the incident was quickly made clear. Three members of the IZL were then in prison. They had been sentenced to hang by a British court for terrorist activities. The IZL were determined to prevent the hangings and had made it clear that if the sentences were not commuted they would kidnap three British soldiers and hang them as reprisal.

Security throughout Palestine was stepped up. Fewer and fewer British troops moved about openly unless they were in groups. Then, on 12 July, two sergeants from the Intelligence Corps went for an evening drink unarmed and in civilian clothes to a café in Nathanya. They had with them a Jewish friend employed by the Army. They were kidnapped by the IZL, and taken to a hiding place which had been prepared beforehand to hold such prisoners. The makeshift cell was under the floor of a factory. It was equipped with a canvas bucket as latrine, held what was considered enough food and water for several days, and had an oxygen cylinder by which the air could be made more breathable.

These two young sergeants were left in this cell without light or sound, and with little hope for their future. An intensive search was organized by the British Military without success. Covert operations also met with no success and on 29 July, in spite of active worldwide protests by Zionist supporters, the three IZL men in Acre Prison were hanged. It is only fair to say that the milder Zionist factions called on the IZL not to exact the reprisal they had promised and hang the two English sergeants.

Within the next twenty-four hours IZL took the two Englishmen – Sergeants Martin and Paice – out of their cell, tied their hands behind their backs with telegraph wire and then hanged them both. The bodies were then cut down, taken to a eucalyptus grove and hung from two trees. A land mine was placed in the ground beneath the spot where the bodies were hanging. IZL also published a notice proclaiming that appeals for clemency had been rejected and that their sentence had been carried out. The two dead bodies were found on the morning of 31 July and a party of troops was sent to collect the corpses.

As the first sergeant was being cut down the rope parted and the soldier who cut the rope jumped clear. The body fell on the mine and was blown into unrecognizable pieces. The explosion also brought down the tree on which the second body was hanging.

Anti-semitic disorder broke out in various parts of England and the police and army in Palestine took the law into their own hands and killed or beat Jews in various villages. By the time control was reimposed, five Jews had been killed and many more injured, but no action was taken against the culprits as they could not officially be identified.

Had it not been for the timely arrival of the armoured cars that scared off the terrorists who held up my driver and me, we might well have suffered the same death, for the IZL said they would hang three British soldiers, but had only captured two.

It was during this year that the Government finally authorized tougher undercover operations in Palestine. And the old counter-gang principle, the system of deniable covert operations whereby special units eliminated the opposition, which had been used during the troubles in Ireland in the early 1920s, was revived.

Under Bernard Fergusson, a senior Palestine policeman, highly trained guerrilla fighters from SOE, and other ex-resistance, behind-the-lines and covert organizations, were recruited to operate special units which would contact terrorist groups by infiltration and liquidate them. The most famous of these men was probably Roy Farran, a highly decorated SAS hero.

However, in spite of the resulting increase in killings on both sides, it became clear that the problem was insoluble. Ernest Bevin's policy of non-participation was again approved at the end of 1947 and it was decided that British rule would end in May 1948. The conflict between the Arabs and the Jews, a bloody conflict, continues to this day.

CHAPTER 5

THERE WERE AT THIS time an enormous number of disaffected German prisoners-of-war held in Egypt, and it soon became clear to the Arabs in Palestine that many of these prisoners not only had outstanding knowledge and experience of weapons and explosives, but were either sympathetic to the Arab cause or, if not that, then anti-semitic in outlook.

Thus started a recruitment programme of Germans by the Arab underground, which began to organize the escape of Germans from their prisoner-of-war camps. These men were then channelled along an escape line to Arab groups operating in Palestine.

What was needed to counter this move was somebody who would work from the inside of the German and Arab operation, in order to break it up.

My fluent German and my ability to pass as a German or a Swiss led inevitably to the job falling on me. So I returned to Egypt to the Canal Zone, which was where most of the German POW camps were situated.

By this time Maurice Oldfield had returned to the United Kingdom and had been demobilized. He immediately took up a position together with Douglas Roberts in MI6, where I continued to keep in touch with him. It soon became my ambition to work for him again within that most secretive organization.

I was established in the Canal Zone in a small unit at Kabrit in what had formerly been a special forces training unit. We were just across the battered tarmac road that led down to Kabrit Point from a small RAF base. Kabrit Point itself thrust into the bitter lakes and held a light as navigation point for the ships passing through the bitter lakes as part of their transit of the Suez Canal.

It was clear to the Arabs, from 1947 on, that they were going to have to fight the Jews in Palestine, and they sought to acquire arms in any way they could.

Arms had been stolen regularly from British depots throughout the Middle East from the end of the war, but this was stepped up in 1947 as German prisoners-of-war began to be used in Egypt to help steal the armaments required. The weapons were then carried across the Sinai on camel back into the hands of escaped German POW instructors, who trained the various Arab units.

We decided that this network had to be broken up as a matter of urgency, so I agreed to be planted in a cell used for interrogating recaptured escapee prisoners to see if I could discover any leads which would enable us to close down the arms pipeline.

I was dressed for the part in blue denim shirt and shorts, with blue diamond patches and a pair of wooden clogs, and, of course, a home-made Afrika Korps peaked cap fashioned from the grey denim of the uniform. My cell mate was Willi Steinhauer who had twice escaped from his camp and twice been recaptured. We knew he must be a mine of information about the various escape routes and techniques.

We were put together in a concrete cell about 10 feet wide by 14 feet long. The ceiling was about 10 feet high, and just below it on one side was a small gap to let in air.

We ate rough bread with water for breakfast, a sort of thin stew for lunch and bread again in the evening. The cooking was done by other German prisoners and we were guarded by black Basuto soldiers of the King's African Rifles, who carried their rifles with bayonets fixed and were not above urging prisoners along to the latrine or the shower with a prod from the sharpened tip of a bayonet.

All prisoners were interrogated regularly, so I was able to talk with my colleagues when necessary without other prisoners becoming aware of my true identity.

The interrogations were in no way physically brutal. The worst that happened was that a recalcitrant interrogatee would be deprived of his bed and also of sleep by having the cement floor of his cell doused with buckets of cold water at regular intervals. And I did hear from other prisoners that some interrogators placed a steel bucket over a man's head and beat it with a broomstick.

After a couple of weeks I came up with two useful pieces of information. One was the address of a restaurant in Suez which was the start of an escape line to Arab Palestine. The other was the name of a prisoner working at an RAF unit near Ismailia, who was involved in the theft of military materials. I passed on this information. The next morning there was a great commotion as I was hauled roughly out of my cell, with soldiers kicking at me and shouting that I was to be taken to court martial for crimes I had committed during my last escape!

After a long hot shower, a shave and a decent meal that didn't involve gruel or bread, I got down to planning how to exploit my two pieces of information.

I decided to start with the escape line in Suez. I acquired some shabby civilian clothes and went down to Suez to recce the Kit-Kat bar which was housed in the less than savoury port area. It appeared to be a fairly standard greasy-spoon type restaurant, with a bar which catered mainly for sailors from the many ships in port. By watching quietly for a couple of days I also determined who visited it regularly and that there were rooms above the restaurant, in which the professional ladies of Suez entertained their clients by the half hour.

Then early one day I went round to the local headquarters of the Military Police in Suez and arranged for a couple of foot patrols to visit a variety of sleazy cafés and restaurants in Suez that afternoon, show a photograph of me in civilian clothes and ask whether I had been seen. They were then to enjoin the proprietors of the various establishments to contact the Military Police should I appear, on pain of having their premises closed down if they did not. To maintain my disguise I reluctantly left my green card and Beretta with the police for safe keeping.

After these suitable preparations I waited for evening and then slunk into the Kit-Kat. Edging my way to the crowded bar, I ordered a beer in my best guttural English. Within a short time the Arab proprietor was standing at the other side of the bar politely inviting me to have a further drink. 'Where have you come from?' he asked.

From his controlled reaction to my presence, I knew he had already decided I was the man the Military Police were looking for. I sought to look somewhat embarrassed and edgy and explained briefly that I was half-German and half-Swiss and that I would be in Suez for a short while. I was making an obvious effort to avoid explaining how I got there, and it worked. The proprietor told me quietly that the British Military Police were looking for somebody whose description tallied exactly with mine and he wondered whether I would not prefer to go into his office for privacy and a further drink, since he thought it not unlikely that the Military Police might return – and that would be embarrassing for everybody.

I made out that I was grateful but also let him see I was suspicious. All the same, I joined him in his office.

Coffee was brought and he then announced, 'I know your name. You're Paul Wagner, an escaped German prisoner-of-war, on the run, and the Military Police are hunting you.' He also announced that he wanted to help me.

I admitted to being Wagner, said I was grateful for his help and asked what he proposed.

In turn, he asked me for some details of my military service and I told him I had been a corporal in the Brandenburger 999 Regiment, a special forces unit which also had a penal battalion. He asked me my age and while today I look considerably younger than my actual age, in those days I looked considerably older. I was in fact nineteen but told him I was twenty-three to bear out my story of having been in the German army long enough to have been captured.

My Arab host said he would need two or three days to make the necessary arrangements, and also, I imagine, to find out anything he could about me. Pre-computers, checking up on people was difficult and time-consuming, particularly on such an enormous bunch of people as German prisoners-of-war in Egypt.

An escape bulletin about me had been issued by the Military Police and an Arab clerk working in any British unit would be able to confirm that this was so. There was not much more the proprietor could hope to achieve and anyway I had a couple of battered back-dated letters addressed to me as Kpl Paul Wagner, which I was able to show him.

For three days I stayed next to the working whores in a small room above the restaurant, with excellent food being brought up to me, mainly barbecued lamb, and unlimited Almaza beer.

During this period various Arabs visited me to discuss both the situation of German prisoners-of-war and the general situation in Palestine.

'Sooner or later the British will go,' I was told time and again, 'and then we will destroy the Jews by force. Believe us, we shall drive them into the sea.'

I was told too that they had been amassing arms ever since the end of the war, and even before that, during the war, from the troops of the 9th Army and those moving through Palestine to the British Forces in Persia. They warned me, however, that some of these weapons were in bad condition because they had been stored without proper care in wells and caves and wadis.

Finally I was asked whether I would be prepared to contact other German POWs who might have access to arms, particularly to hand grenades, ammunition and Sten guns. After discussion and a promise of both considerable funds and of help with my escape, I agreed to work with them.

Reasonable but over-dressy civilian clothes were obtained for me, I shaved, made myself look as presentable as possible and on the evening before I was to leave we had a last conference in the brothel upstairs. I was given five hundred Egyptian pounds and a seaman's identity card which showed me to be a Norwegian. I arranged to meet Mustapha, one of the Arabs who had visited, two weeks later at a marker stone ten kilometres out of Ismailia on the Canal road, going south.

Wearing my pimp's suit and with my Norwegian identity, I took leave of my new Arab friends and walked to the Suez bus depot to board an ancient bus bound for Fayed and Fanara. As soon as I got past Shandur I kept my eyes open for the white-cabbed trucks of 804 Company RASC. This was an expanded British transport company operated entirely by Germans. There were four or five British officers and about ten British NCOs under a sergeant-major. The remainder of the 800-strong Company were Germans. Not surprisingly, it was probably the most efficient unit in the British Army at that time.

The workshops could carry out any repair on almost any

vehicle and their Dodge trucks had a lower off-the-road time than did most similar vehicles in British hands.

As I came closer to the unit's camp I left the ramshackle bus at a small Arab tea bar much used by German drivers. I soon got into conversation with a couple of unshaven 804 drivers who rapidly saw through my disguise as a Norwegian, but were anxious to help a fellow POW on the run. I met them on three subsequent days for a cup of dark coffee, all the time learning more and more about their duties.

Eventually one of them mentioned that they frequently went to 108 MU, an RAF camp outside Ismailia. I asked them if they had made friends there with any of the Germans who were employed in the Stores. When they said yes, I took the plunge and assured them that there was good money available if any arms could be stolen and smuggled out of the camp. With the war already two years gone, every German was anxious to get home. This was almost always possible provided the person had access to reasonable amounts of money; several hundred pounds was then considered a reasonable amount. We agreed to meet a week later and I left to hide myself in a small dark hotel in the back streets of Ismailia.

A week later I returned by broken-down bus and again met the two men. They told me that it would be possible to steal hand grenades with detonators, and also .303 ammunition. When I asked them in what quantities, they told me as much as a 15-cwt truck could carry.

I was now ready to report to Mustapha and told my German friends that I would meet them again in the same café a week later. Then I returned to Ismailia and killed time unobtrusively as I waited for the arrival of the fourteenth day since leaving Suez.

A bus dropped me off near the ninth kilometre marker stone out of Ismailia, and I started walking slowly along at the side of the dusty road towards kilometre stone number ten. Once I got there I looked round for a suitable place to sit in the shade and noticed a clump of palm trees fifty or sixty paces off the road. Exactly on time Mustapha arrived, driving in a large but rather battered green Chrysler, and seeing me beckoned for me to join him. I ran over, clambered in and we clattered off down the

30

road until we were able to park discreetly by the side of the Suez Canal.

I reported to Mustapha that I had indeed found some Germans who were able to steal a truck load of grenades and ammunition and his face lit up with joy. We sketched out a plan and agreed to meet again at the same place in two days' time, when he would bring £1000 which I was to divide between the German who organized the theft of the weapons and the driver who would bring the stores to a rendezvous that Mustapha would arrange. He had brought £500 for me, which I happily accepted.

Our plan was as follows. On the following Wednesday morning a truck would pull out of 108 MU laden with the stolen goods with only the driver aboard. The truck would drive sedately towards Ismailia, and at kilometre four I would be waiting. I would then brief the driver on what to do from then on. I warned Mustapha that the man back in the camp would be unlikely to agree to load up the truck until he saw the £500 he was to get, and so we agreed that I should pass on half of the £500 I had just been given to show good will, and the loader's balance would be given to the driver along with his own £500 when the goods were delivered.

The Wednesday morning dawned hot and sticky and, at the time expected, the 804 Company Dodge rumbled up to the arranged kilometre stone where I was waiting. I climbed in and gave the necessary instructions, which were to drive to the next kilometre stone where a young Arab boy should be waiting. The boy was to ask if we could give him a lift as he had lost a shoe.

We found the boy waiting with his one shoe and sat him in the cab between us. At his direction we drove almost into Ismailia and then turned off towards a busy sand pit. There we transferred the arms from the Dodge to a gaily-painted local carrier's truck. I then handed the money over to the driver and we went our separate ways.

During the time I had been lying low in Ismailia I had kept in touch with the local ADSO and the Officer-in-Charge of the Field Security Station, whose offices were quite close to the French Club, which had what was undoubtedly one of the best restaurants in Egypt. I had carefully kept these two gentlemen informed of any arrangements that had been made, both with Mustapha and the Germans, and had agreed that from the moment we picked up the Arab boy our truck was to be shadowed. Once the handover of the arms was made to the Arab truck, the Arab truck would be halted by two armoured cars, the contents of the truck retrieved and the Arabs arrested.

So later that Wednesday morning I returned to my sleazy hotel, tried to smarten myself up, and, checking that I was not being followed, walked swiftly round to the Field Security Office to see how the arrest had gone. The mortification felt by those in the Field Security Office and by myself when we discovered that the shadowing of the German truck had failed and there had been no arrest was unprintable. The Arabs had thus made off with 15 cwt of grenades and ammunition for which we were accountable to the Commanding Officer of 108 MU, since it was 'arranged' with him that they could be stolen – and now we had lost them.

The only link in the whole process, the only clue, was my description of the Arab truck and the young boy who had met me on the Canal road.

The ADSO immediately summoned Riad Bey, the Senior Officer in the Egyptian Police, and we bundled into the ADSO's smart Mercury convertible. The ADSO, Riad, another police officer and myself prowled the back streets of Ismailia hoping against hope we might see the boy or the truck.

I saw the boy.

Riad and his colleague jumped out of the car and grabbed the boy. They dragged him into the car and we drove as quickly as possible to Police Headquarters. There we all bundled into an interrogation room where the poor child was stripped of everything but his shoes and given a beating before even being asked any questions.

The boy angrily denied all knowledge of me and of the arms in question and Riad asked me if I was sure it was the boy. I said I was, and the naked boy was then lifted on to a table where he was held down by three brawny Egyptian police. One of these removed the boy's shoes and began to whip the soles of his feet with a thin metal rod until, through the boy's screams and sobs, came the information Riad needed. The carrier's truck had taken the stolen

32

goods to a small village just outside Ismailia where they had been hidden in a dry well. We rushed off to the village accompanied by a lorry load of armed police, while the poor boy who could no longer walk was dragged along as our guide.

As we roared into the village everybody scattered and the police took up position with their rifles at the port around the well, and while Riad summoned the head man, one of the policemen climbed down into the well and announced that the boxes of military stores were there.

This operation later led to the arrest of all the Arabs on the Egyptian side of the pipeline shipping arms up to Palestine. They were arrested by the Egyptian Police on the basis of the initial information given by the boy, and were secured out of harm's way in the appalling conditions of an Egyptian prison.

However, the immediate problem we all faced was deciding when the news of the arrest of the Arab group, including Mustapha, would be most likely to reach the Kit-Kat bar in Suez, and, as a consequence, 'blow' me as a *Spitzel*, a stool-pigeon.

In the end we decided that if we moved quickly we could risk following through. We decided not to arrest the Germans who were involved in the weapon stealing until the second part of my mission in Suez was accomplished.

I took the old battered desert bus back to Suez and arrived the following evening. I was welcomed warmly by the café proprietor and, after I'd returned to the same upstairs room, he came up for a discussion. I told him that I had arranged for an arms transaction which had been completed yesterday, and that I'd also found three prisoners who were willing, if their escape was aided, to go to Palestine as weapon instructors. I said I wanted to leave early next morning and go back to Fayed and advise these three on where they should make contact after they had left their camps.

The café owner hurried out saying he would return immediately, and I attacked a large portion of lamb kebab and prayed that I would be able to get out of the Kit-Kat alive before news of the Ismailia disaster reached the ears of those in whose midst I now found myself. If I did not, I had no doubt I would end up as another bloated corpse floating face down in the Canal.

I slept badly that night, waking early in a sweat. In fact, pistol in hand, I crept down the stairs at about four in the morning and left, suddenly having had an intuitive feeling that all was definitely not well.

I waited silently in the shadow of a shop doorway about fifty yards down the narrow street and soon found my intuitive feeling had been correct. Around an hour later, just as the sun was beginning to rise, a large American car drew up outside the Kit-Kat and the café proprietor and two hefty-looking brethren clambered out and went into the Kit-Kat. The minute they disappeared inside I set off at full speed for the Military Police Office, where I was able to put on my own clothes and tidy myself up; ending up looking more like a respectable civilian and less like a Greek pimp.

Although I regarded my part in this operation as finishing rather ignobly, by keeping the place under observation we were eventually able to establish the route which the POWs were taking to Palestine and, in due course, the route was shut down. It was in connection with this that I made the trip to Palestine which resulted in the severe battering that I took at the hands of the IZL.

My time in the Army in the Middle East between July 1946 and July 1948 was spent mainly in Egypt and Palestine. However, on two occasions I was 'lent' to other intelligence units to help them out. I conducted some interrogations of Jewish illegal immigrants in Cyprus, as the Russians were suspected of planting people amongst the Jewish refugees seeking to get to Palestine, and when these agents were detected they were subjected to intense interrogation.

I also paid a visit to Salonica in northern Greece where deserters from the Communist side during the Greek Civil War were held. We had already started collecting Soviet and Soviet-satellite order of battle information, which the line-crossers (particularly those from Bulgaria) gave us.

This was my introduction to 'civilian' intelligence work. For two years I had been in the Middle East in Egypt, Palestine, Cyprus and Greece. In retrospect, and in view of what I was to learn in MI6, it was really low-level to middle-level work, and those of us who worked with MI6 officers knew that that organization was the tops and that they – not us – were the real professionals.

At one time I had been offered the post of G3I (General Staff Officer Grade 3) with the 6th Airborne Division in Palestine. But this would have taken me back to regimental soldiering, and, although I was operating for intelligence at a fairly junior level, at least I had a great deal of control over my actions and activity. As the time for my demobilization approached, I handed over my various projects.

On a beautiful summer's day I steamed out of Port Said on what was really a luxury cruise to Marseilles, and then carried on by train across France, eventually reaching a demobilization centre where I was given a pair of grey flannel trousers and a ghastly light blue and brown sports jacket. With these and several weeks' pay, which was at the rate of about thirty shillings a day, I left the Army and immediately took four weeks' holiday in Switzerland. I was already clear in my own mind that what I wanted most to do was to carry on in the intelligence world and if possible with Maurice in MI6.

CHAPTER 6

I NEVER APPRECIATED SWITZERLAND as much as I did in those four weeks of holiday; and it was to be a long time before I had that amount of holiday again.

The contrast of England both in wartime and even then in 1948, still subject to shortages and with the scars of war still visible and the regulated life of Army service, with Switzerland made the sparkle, cleanliness and plenty a joy. I walked daily in the mountains and spent my time with various other young people who were also having their first holiday since the war.

In September I was back in London preparing to attend an interview at what was then called 'Intelligence Coordination Staff'. I had already received a letter which said, 'We understand you might be interested in government service involving periods of work abroad. We should be obliged if you would come for an interview at Princes Gate, SW7 at 3 o'clock on the afternoon of ...'

I knew already from Maurice that this was the beginning of my being looked over for an appointment with MI6. With as much spit and polish as I could muster, I reported on time at the place mentioned, and after barely a minute's wait was ushered into a large room and asked to sit down on a chair facing a mahogany table. Behind the table were seated five middle-aged men. I was later to discover that the chairman of the group, who sat in the middle of the five, was Captain Frank Slocum, RN, who during the war had run a hotchpotch fleet of yachts and fishing boats carrying agents into Europe. Another man on the interviewing committee was Dick Brooman-White, formerly Head of the MI6 station in Turkey, and later to become a Member of Parliament. I believe one of the others on the Board was Tony Milne, then Deputy Head of R5.

The questions put to me that afternoon, mainly by Slocum but occasionally by one of the others, related to my childhood in Switzerland and my service to date in the Army. After all, that just about covered my life until then. I was questioned more than once about a close family friend who I had given as a reference, and who was then a Senior Officer of the Trades Union Congress, and I was asked to outline what I wanted to do now that I had left the Army.

I explained that I had liked working in intelligence and hoped that I might continue in it. To this end I hoped my fluency with languages and my ability to get on with foreigners might prove useful. However, if this were not possible I felt my talents might be equally useful in a journalistic capacity. The interview lasted roughly an hour, with nobody having explained to me who the gentlemen interviewing me were, nor which particular department of government they represented.

I found out later that many people who went for this sort of interview never realized they were being interviewed for the Secret Service. There were even those who were recruited into the Service but did not realize until after they had completed a week or two's work in Broadway Buildings in St James's, which used to be the Headquarters of MI6. One thing they did tell me at the interview was that for the job they had in mind there was a minimum age limit of twenty-five and, therefore, the fact that I was only just twenty-one would probably count against me.

While I was conceited enough to feel that I ought to be accepted into intelligence, I nevertheless made the rounds of the newspaper offices seeking a job as a trainee reporter.

The most helpful person I came across was Hugh Chevins, Industrial Correspondent of the *Daily Telegraph*. He told me only what other people in Fleet Street had already told me, that I should first get some experience on a provincial paper and then come back to London. Chevins did, however, say that I could come and be a sort of glorified office boy in his department for the princely sum of £4 10s a week.

We agreed that I should start with the *Daily Telegraph* on 1 November, by which time I secretly hoped to be in MI6. Two weeks after my meeting with Chevins I received another letter from the Intelligence Coordination Staff and this one asked me to attend a language test.

I was ushered into another large room in which a most distinguished man sat in solitary splendour, dressed in a dark blue double-breasted suit, highly polished black shoes and with sleek brushed-down white hair. I later discovered that he was the Count van den Heuvel, known throughout the Service either as Fanny or by his symbol Z: he was a close friend of the current Head of the Secret Service and had been the head of its wartime operations in Switzerland. (He was also Managing Director of Eno's Fruit Salts!)

Fanny said that he understood I spoke German, French and Swiss-German and he had been asked to test me.

We started off in Swiss-German, which soon became a bit of a joke. Fanny had a reputation of being a brilliant Swiss-German speaker and spoke that 'throat illness' of a language as well as a third-year French student would speak French in an English school. After a few minutes he announced there was no point in us going on, and that he had never heard an Englishman speak Swiss-German so well.

That evening I discussed both my previous interview and this language test with Maurice Oldfield over dinner at Schmidts in Charlotte Street. Maurice told me that he anticipated I would be accepted into the Service and, if that were so, I would be its youngest officer.

A few days later I received a letter, again from ICS, advising me that as a result of my interview I was offered employment as a junior officer liable to serve from time to time overseas at a starting salary of £400 per year. If I wished to accept this employment, I should acknowledge this letter in writing and report to the office where I had been originally interviewed, at 9.30 the following Monday morning.

The first thing I did on arrival that Monday morning was to sign the Official Secrets Act, after which I was told to report to an establishment officer at 54 Broadway. So I became a member of the Secret Intelligence Service, otherwise known as SIS or MI6,[1] or

[1] MI6 is the Military Intelligence cover designation and descends from the foreign section of the Secret Service Bureau, which moved into the War Office in October 1909, under the legendary Mansfield Smith-Cumming.

informally as the Firm or the Friends. We were known by MI5 at that time as 'the people across the park'. I was told in the Establishment Department that I would work in R5 and was sent up to Maurice Oldfield's room. By working for him again, and this time in the most professional of British intelligence services, I had finally achieved the ambition I had nurtured since I had first met Maurice in Cairo. I was pleased that note had obviously been taken of my languages, since I was to work in the section dealing with counterespionage in Germany, Austria and Switzerland.

The Chief of MI6 was Major General Sir Stewart Menzies, whom I had never met but whom I saw on a couple of occasions when I walked along the passages of the fourth floor, which housed the suites of the top three men in the Service. Under him the Service divided into two, the production side under the Vice Chief, General Sir John Sinclair, and the requirement side under the Assistant Chief, Air Commodore (later Sir) Jack Easton.

The production side produced the intelligence the customers required and the requirement side processed the information and safeguarded the sources when passing it on to the customers.

The customers were various ministries and departments in Whitehall and they all had a link to one of the requirement or R sections.

Thus R1 dealt with political information and the Foreign Office, R2 with air information and the Air Ministry, R3 with naval information and the Admiralty, R4 with military information and the War Office, and R5 with counterespionage information and information on subversion and communism. R5 was therefore in itself a consumer of information and a customer in its own right.

R5's other customers were MI5 and certain allied foreign intelligence services.

R6 dealt with economic information and worked with the Treasury, the Bank of England and the Board of Trade.

At the end of 1915, SIS was renamed MI(1)C. It was transferred to the overall control of the Foreign Office in 1917. In 1919 the Cabinet gave MI5 responsibility for counterespionage in the United Kingdom and her overseas interests, and the Secret Intelligence Service (now called MI6) responsibility for all intelligence matters in areas of the world outside the Empire.

R7 dealt with scientific information and was also known as TAL (Tube Alloys Liaison), which was the department working in the nuclear field.

R8 dealt with GCHQ at Cheltenham.

The production side was divided up into country areas which worked through production sections for each country and the regional controllers who came under chief controllers. These chief controllers divided the world up into areas with a Chief Controller Europe, a Chief Controller Mediterranean and a Chief Controller Pacific. There was a similar ranking officer in charge of the Americas.

Each of the P (production) sections was responsible for one or more operating stations abroad. Thus, in dealing with Germany, Austria or Switzerland, I had to deal with the P section handling those countries. The P section was responsible for seeing that the various stations and networks they controlled were in a position to provide the information that each of the requirement departments needed.

For example, if the War Office (MoD) required to know whether a new type of Soviet tank shown off at a May Day Parade in Moscow was yet in service in Eastern Germany, the officer in the Directorate of Military Intelligence (today MoD) responsible for this wrote a brief for R4 and gave it to the officer in that section with whom he normally liaised. Having got the brief, the Army officer attached to SIS to make up the R4 section, would discuss the requirement with the P section officer, who would then send out a request to the overseas station most likely to be able to provide the answer.

In normal circumstances a request like this would go to the Berlin station and be handed to the case officer who handled an agent who was either a specialist in military matters, or who had access to the part of East Germany where the tanks were thought to be. When, in due course, the agent reported back – possibly with a sketch or even a photograph – the information was passed back to the R4 officer who had originated the enquiry.

The R4 officer would know the full details of the source, but he would not reveal these to his customer in the War Office. He would pass the information over under the cover of a source sheet, which would give some details of the source; saying perhaps that the source was a farm labourer who worked on land adjoining a tank training ground, that he had been our agent for two years and that his information was usually 80 per cent reliable.

The customer would then be asked to report back on the accuracy and usefulness of the information after he had compared it with whatever other information he had.

The same system applied to all the other R departments except R5, which was a law unto itself being its own customer. Douglas Roberts, who had been Head of SIME and my Brigadier when I first arrived in Cairo, was now the Head of R5. Under him was a deputy, Tony Milne, who had sat on my entrance selection board. Then the department divided into two equal parts. One dealt with counterintelligence under Maurice Oldfield, and the other with the investigation of communism. This last group was headed by Charles Ransom, later to become one of the authors of the *Official History of British Wartime Intelligence*. Both sides of R5 were broken down into country sections, so that as far as Germany, Austria and Switzerland were concerned, there was one officer studying Russian and satellite intelligence service activities in those countries, and one officer studying the action of the communist and communist front organizations in those territories, to whom I was initially attached.

CHAPTER 7

IN OCTOBER 1948, WHEN I had barely been in MI6 a month, there was an urgent demand for officers with fluent German to handle a sudden increase in information relating to communist political activity. This arose because part of the Control Commission's intelligence arm had been brought under the control of SIS. I was therefore loaned to the German station for a couple of months to help process the rising backlog of information.

On my return to the UK I was sent on an intelligence course, known as the General Trade Craft Course, which lasted eight weeks. It was held in an old building in Palace Street, close to a pub called The Albert which we used regularly, and which still stands, although the remainder of Palace Street has been redeveloped.

We assembled that first Monday at 10 o'clock and took a good look at each other. There were twenty-four of us and we were divided into six groups of four. The most senior officer was a tanned middle-aged colonial called John, who permanently wore battered suede shoes. While I was the youngest, I was certainly not the most junior, for some of the students were on the course within a week of joining the Service. Our course director was a moon-faced smiling man, also a suede-shoe wearer, called Tony. He explained briefly that we were divided into syndicates and that in the various coming exercises the syndicates would be pitted against each other.

As some of the exercises would continue from one day to another, we were each given a box file which we were told to consider as being 'a diplomatic bag', into which any notes or papers relating to the exercise could be put overnight – and once they were in these boxes we were to regard them as being inviolate. Some of our exercises involved shadowing or being shadowed through the streets of the West End, and we soon discovered that the best way in which to lose a follower was by hopping into Peter Jones or the old Swan and Edgar. There were also exercises in making contact with an 'agent' at a given rendezvous and at a given time with necessary recognition signals and passwords. Methods had not changed much – and still haven't – from those used for wartime SOE meetings, where the person to be contacted would carry a copy of a certain newspaper in the left hand and a rolled umbrella in the right hand, and stand under a given lamppost at a given place.

The contact would approach and ask the direction to x and y.

To which the first person would reply, 'I live at number 24, which number are you looking for?'

When the contact replied with the correct number, contact had been made.

We also travelled down to Fort Monkton at Gosport, where longer courses in weapons and explosives were held.

We had long lectures on famous examples of agent handling and innumerable discussion sessions in which problems were raised and we were invited to solve them.

Two of the officers on the course were women and were, in fact, promoted secretaries. Both of them were extremely competent and both, in due course, became heads of station. One of them was later to help me greatly during the Hungarian revolution, when she was based in the Embassy in Budapest.

I was sometimes surprised by the innocence of some of the people recruited by SIS. One of the syndicates contained a new entrant who the hierarchy obviously thought had some qualities, since he had been recruited straight from the Indian Police. An early exercise involved each syndicate being pitted against the other five in an exercise that lasted for four days.

On the evening of the last day of the exercise I went back to our building in Palace Street and, on the pretence of having misplaced a valuable cigarette lighter, asked the security guard to let me into the building. Since, in any event, I had an SIS pass which gave me admission at all times, the door was opened for me and I immediately went up to our lecture room, opened the cupboard that contained the sacred boxes, and memorized the plans and proposals of the other five syndicates.

On the last day, when the solutions to the problem were given, it was obvious that our syndicate knew beforehand what the other five syndicates were planning, because we had a counter for each of their moves. It was therefore also obvious to everyone that somebody in our group had violated the secure box files.

I promptly admitted that it was I, and told them how I had done so. It was plain from the way our instructors reacted that they felt it showed initiative and that they had expected somebody to violate the boxes.

Not so our Indian Police officer, who stood up white with anger and said that this was 'not cricket', and that he no longer wished to be associated with such people. He resigned at no great loss to a service which has to be prepared to go to any lengths to achieve its objects.

On completion of the Field Craft Course I returned to R5 and was given my own desk with responsibility for counterespionage in Germany, Austria and Switzerland. Seventy per cent of this work involved studying, assessing and penetrating the Russian intelligence services and 25 per cent involved the satellite intelligence services. The remainder related to work with friendly foreign intelligence services. Most of the results of our endeavours were shared with MI5 with whom we then worked very closely.

My early arrogance towards M15 was quickly sat on by an older officer, Bobby Silem, who when I asked 'How rude can we be to MI5?', sent me off to Maurice for a severe dressing down.

In addition to my desk work, I was given a most interesting assignment. One of the earliest important defectors from the Soviet Union was Lieutenant Colonel Grigori Tokaev, a brilliant aeronautical scientist in the Soviet Air Force. Shortly after his defection, he had been spirited away from his first base in Germany and now lived in a safe house in the suburbs of London with his wife and small daughter.

He was obviously of enormous value both to the Air Force and to our aeronautical design people, for this was at the time that the MIG-15 Soviet fighter was astounding Western aviation experts with its performance. But, quite apart from his value to the aviation boys, it was extremely beneficial for us to have a senior Russian Staff Officer with whom we could discuss Russian military ways and techniques.

There were two reasons for my being given the job of working with Tokaev. Firstly, I was the Task Officer for the activities of the KGB[1] in Germany, and secondly Tokaev spoke good German so we had a common language. Once a week I would indent for a self-drive office car and travel down to Tokaev's suburban house. If the weather was bad we would sit in his small drawing room, and if it was warm we would drive to a nearby park and stroll over the grass talking about his life in the Russian Air Force, about senior officers he knew and their views and, of course, about anything he knew of Soviet intelligence.

Tokaev also had a regular Case Officer, an émigré officer who spoke Russian. I rapidly developed a close relationship with Tokaev and found him a warm and friendly man but, like most defectors, anxious to be seen to be more important than he was.

R5 section had a great deal to do with the CIA station in London, the prime objective of which was to liaise with British Services. The Head of London Station was Winston Scott, a cheerful and pleasant former Naval Commander who subsequently retired to Mexico City, where he died only a few years ago. Whenever Winston and his colleagues visited our offices, they were always greeted with the friendly greeting, 'Hi, turn your papers over, the Yanks are coming.'

I had a somewhat wild social life at the time, as there were a number of beautiful young women in the office, most of whom seemed to be the daughters of senior services officers, and all of whom had been recruited by personal contact. Most of them lived in a hostel in Cromwell Road, run by the Service, which was supervised by an SIS matron, an old dragon who was supposed to keep them out of mischief.

As they were repeatedly briefed to be extremely careful with whom they associated, they consequently felt secure only when they were in the company of people doing the same work. From their first day in the office they were assessed, just as officers were,

---

[1] MGB at the time, but I have used KGB for ease of reference throughout.

for their suitability for posting abroad in an embassy. When I was eventually posted to Germany in the summer of 1950, I already knew and had worked with a large number of those who now worked at the German station.

My ignorance of ultra-professional intelligence operations had been brought home to me by those original two months in Germany, and I vowed from that time on to absorb the moral of the old Russian story given at the beginning of this book.

To take up that summer posting in Germany I set off from Northolt Airfield near London and flew in an RAF Dakota to Buckeberg, one of the principal RAF transport fields in West Germany. A young and very obviously British driver in tweed jacket and flannels stood by a black Humber Super Snipe, one of the most powerful and fastest British production cars at that time. It was quite clear who had come to meet me!

What comedy of errors arranged for the Secret Service in Germany to be supplied with a fleet of those distinctive cars I never established, but suffice it to say that it did not take long for anyone sufficiently interested to realize that where there was a black Humber Super Snipe, the British Secret Service was at work. The driver who met me was called Harry and he later became the driver I used whenever I needed a big and fast car. It has to be remembered that, in those days, our operations in Germany were paid for out of occupation costs and each officer was therefore issued with his own Volkswagen Beetle. These were embellished in various ways, either by painting them a colour other than black, or by fitting badges, spotlights, radios and so on. A wide selection of different number plates was also available to us.

My cover in Germany was as an officer of the Control Commission, and indeed nearly all SIS officers and secretaries had this or military cover.

As well as our headquarters in a small spa town not far from Bielefeld, we had outstations in Berlin, Hamburg, Hanover, Düsseldorf and Frankfurt and there was a one-man operation in Munich.

During this period Germany was the advance base of the Cold War against the Soviet bloc and with the enormous numbers of SIS officers in Germany, probably fifty with a back-up staff (drivers, secretaries, quartermasters) of a further two hundred or so, this operation was almost as big as SIS itself.

Also operating in Germany was the Intelligence Divison of the Control Commission, and the British Army, Air Force and Navy also had their intelligence functions. Each of the four allies had a mission attached to each other's headquarters. In Berlin there was Brixmis (the British Mission to the Soviet Commander-in-Chief), an organization made up of service officers whose job it was to liaise with the Soviet forces. As a consequence, they had a right to travel throughout divided Germany, including the Russian zone, and not surprisingly, they did more observing than liaising with the Soviet armed forces, being able to travel virtually anywhere while armed with cameras. It was also not surprising that they wer often chased and equally often arrested by the Soviet authorities. The head of the entire SIS operation was Big John, an officer who had been in SIS throughout most of the war and before that had served in the Middle East and Paris. Below him was Little John, who was Station Commander for all Germany, and below him came the Outstation Commanders.

A postwar change in the symbols used to designate foreign countries meant that Germany became BAH and the chief representative in Germany was known as BAH 51.

Each of the heads of the outstations took a different symbol: Berlin was BAH 01 and most of the remaining officers were BAH 02–A, B, C and then on to 02–AA, AB, AC until everybody had a symbol. Thus the head of the station's secretary became BAH 51 Sec., and every secretary carried the symbol of the officer she worked for.

Apart from the officers and secretaries, there was a complete support operation of drivers, clerks, storemen, workshops, bat-men, safe-housekeepers and officers' mess staff. The most menial jobs were done by civilians, either German or displaced persons under British supervision. Nobody really thought that our cover was very good, but it gave us all a reason for being in Germany, even though I am sure that few who needed to know were fooled. Our messes, where the officers and secretaries lived – and which, were, of course, single sex – were run at a far higher standard than any others, and while other Control Commission people shared messes, SIS messes were for SIS only.

On arrival at Headquarters I went first to the mess for bachelor officers where I was to live. Most of the married officers were accompanied by their wives and had luxurious (requisitioned) houses staffed by maids and cooks.

This life in Germany gave rise to a Service myth that the basic difference between the cover of an SIS officer and his KGB opposite number was summed up by his wife's reaction to a new posting. On learning that they were to be transferred to a new post overseas, the MI6 wife was likely to ask, 'And how many servants will we have, darling?'; whereas the KGB officer's wife would be more likely to enquire, 'Are you going to be a chauffeur again?'

For the good of the Service, senior Russian officers were often posted with menial jobs as cover, while the British officer's, or, perhaps more accurately, his wife's, problem was how the new cover would affect their social status.

Next morning I reported to the office, where I was informed I would be working under Derek – a former thirty-year-old Brigadier – who was now Second-in-Command of the station and whose vivacious wife's main project in life was matching up secretaries and officers. He was later dismissed from the Service for hiding previous Communist Party membership. Initially, I was to work in P section which provided support for agent-running operations. After three months of this, and of travelling around to the various outstations, I was called in one morning to see Big John and told that in the event of war and Soviet occupation of the British zone, there had to be a Service evacuation plan. True, there was a general Control Commission plan, and more particularly an Intelligence Division (known as Int. Div.) evacuation plan, but MI6 needed its own plan either as a back-up or to use instead.

And so I set off on the journey described in chapter 2 and spent in all an interesting three to four weeks exploring the coastline of West Germany, earmarking various local tugs and other suitable vessels for a new Dunkirk should the need arise. I must have completed this job satisfactorily, because I was then given various other responsible jobs – quite often by Big John himself.

It was during this period that the former German General, Reinhard Gehlen, was setting up his American-backed intelligence service in the American zone. Gehlen had already had a fairly successful career in German military intelligence, and had now set up with American support a network of German agents, initially operating in Eastern Germany, and later into the satellites and the Soviet Union itself.[1]

While the British had no say in whom the Americans supported, or what actions they took, we were obviously extremely interested in knowing whether the Russians had targeted in on the Gehlen organization and if so with what success.

One of General Gehlen's secretaries had been recruited to our Service some time previously, and had been run as an agent by Big John. It was to tell me that I was to take over the handling of this agent that Big John next summoned me.

He explained that this was an extremely delicate matter, since it meant contacting the woman in question within the American zone – and if discovered this would prove to be embarrassing. Contacts were therefore always extremely discreet, arranged once a month and each month on the day before that of the previous meeting, so that if we met on a Friday in January the next meeting was on a Thursday in February and so on, omitting weekends. The time was always one hour after sunset and we met in one of three little *Gasthäuser*, where we contrived to give the appearance of a romantic couple.

Our main interest was the use to which the Gehlen organization was putting the League of Free Jurists (FJ). This group of West German lawyers had been set up in 1949 by two West Berliners, Theodore Friedenall and Walter Linse. Although the original job of the FJ was to help people in the Soviet zone with legal advice, this was soon only a cover for what quickly became an efficient intelligence machine.

The FJ Headquarters in West Berlin was in touch with the intelligence services of the three occupying Western powers and, not unnaturally, Gehlen felt he should be in on this, the more so as this was a German group. What Gehlen did not understand was that the FJ considered the British SIS the most efficient of their liaison partners and were reluctant to work with Gehlen's

---

[1] E.H. Cookridge in his book *Gehlen – Spy of the Century* writes extensively on this so there is no need to cover the same ground again.

American-backed intelligence organization. However, in view of the large amounts of money Gehlen's office had at its disposal, the FJ sought to get as much of this as they could in return for as little as they could get away with giving.

The information I obtained from the secretary in the Gehlen organization gave us interesting inside information on the reliability of the FJ people with whom we were dealing.

We were also interested in Radio Free Europe (RFE). Set up in 1949 as an anti-communist broadcast service to the Soviet zone and the satellites, RFE also developed an information department that produced valuable intelligence. Although we had an officer whose specific duties included both liaison with RFE and the exploitation of any leads that came from them, the information I obtained from my new source in the Gehlen organization about their interest in RFE was of benefit in assembling a complete and reliable picture of the situation behind the Iron Curtain.

A further source of good intelligence was the information section of the SDP (the Social Democratic Party). German Social Democrats remained in friendly contact with former comrades in the East who now worked under the umbrella of such communist front organizations as the SED (Socialist Unity Party) and various trade union bodies. So much political information on East Germany became available through these channels that a regional office of SIS was set up in Hanover just to handle this prolific source.

There were also the émigré associations; chief among these were the NTS (People's Labour Alliance) and the various organizations for the Ukrainian and Polish exiles, and those formed by refugees from the Baltic States. I was soon to become very closely involved with the latter. However, I was first to learn of an operation SIS had started and of which, on the present-day basis of 'need to know', I would probably have remained ignorant. I will call it PROJECT.

It has always been extremely difficult to get intelligence out of the Soviet Union, so, with the Cold War at its height, it was decided in 1950 that attempts must be made to contact those resistance movements working against the regime in parts of Soviet Russia.

Most of the intelligence coming out of the Soviet Union via

the émigré organizations was considered suspect for two basic reasons, and all reports of émigré sources were labelled *Mauve*.

The first reason for suspicion was that the various organizations were not primarily set up as intelligence-gathering units and were both insecure and often penetrated by the KGB. Secondly, we found that émigré officers who passed us this information could never refrain from gilding the lily.

So it was that Menzies obtained authority for SIS to train and drop our own agents into the Soviet Union, and PROJECT I, the first such operation, was set up. Agents had to be recruited and trained, then arrangements were made to have them parachuted into the USSR. The officer in charge of this operation was Colonel Harold Gibson, an old hand in SIS who had been Station Commander in Prague at the outbreak of war.

Gibson, known universally in intelligence as 'Gibby', was about fifty-two when I first met him in the summer of 1950. He had been born in Russia, spoke perfect Russian, and had recently married a beautiful blonde White Russian wife with whom he took up residence in our little spa town. His obvious knowledge of Russia and Russians suggested he was probably involved in some operation directed against the Soviet Union, but security was such that initially only those who needed to know knew exactly what he was doing. He had an assistant, a good friend of mine named Terence who was a wartime SOE hero with the Military Cross. Terence was one of the first Russian language students at Cambridge after the war and he too spoke excellent Russian.

At suitable phases of the moon, teams of two or three highly trained agents were dropped into the Ukraine or Byelorussia. I knew that PROJECTS II, III, and IV went ahead and after arrival the dropped agents made radio contact with their base station in Western Germany. However, several of the agents were captured, tried – some in show trials – and then shot. Today I still wonder whether those who did continue in radio contact did so under KGB control.

Another senior officer who turned up in Germany at this time was Colonel Harold Perkins, known, not unnaturally, as 'Perks'. He had managed a coal mine in Poland before the war and had headed the Polish section of SOE. I developed a considerable friendship with him and with Rollo his assistant and their secretary Margo. Although we spent a lot of spare time together, and talked about intelligence matters in general, I never knew what their task was. Years later I found out that they were running the Albanian operation[1] proposed by Julian Amery and our close friend Billy McLean which was to end in failure, probably because of Kim Philby.

The blockade of Berlin convinced Ernest Bevin, the British Foreign Secretary, that the Cold War really was a war, and the first major covert operation he approved was a plan to foment a revolution in Albania which would overthrow the communist dictator Hoxha. Although originally a British plot, the CIA were brought into it; no doubt in view of the expense of the operation. Amery and McLean, who had both been active in the military mission to Albania during the war, felt that one of their partisan contacts Abas Kupi could bring about a rising which would result in Albania becoming a non-communist thorn in the side of the mainly communist Balkans.

A joint SIS/CIA committee to coordinate the operation was established in Washington, and Kim Philby was a member of it. However, while Kim would undoubtedly have informed his Soviet masters of the proposed action, it is also probable that insecure communication blew the operation. Increasing casualties caused the major large-scale operation to be cancelled in the spring of 1950, and thereafter agents were sent in only in ones or twos. It was the first major covert operation since the war and it had failed.

At about the time of this major operation I was handed another task. The police in West Berlin had picked up an East German call girl in West Berlin and promptly discovered the name of a British officer listed in her diary. The officer's name was a common English name, such as John Smith. Big John wanted me to investigate the matter and ascertain whether there was any connection between the 'John Smith' mentioned in the woman's diary and a 'John Smith' who was one of our officers. I was given a *carte blanche* to carry out this investigation, which did not endear

---

[1] This whole operation is discussed in Anthony Verrier's *Through the Looking Glass*, in my opinion the finest book on covert intelligence yet written.

me at all to most of my elder colleagues who resented being questioned by the 'boy of the outfit'.

It was obviously important that a report on as delicate a matter as this should be absolutely impartial, and I therefore studied the rules of evidence as applied at that time in the manual of military law.

My investigation involved bouts of frantic travelling between Berlin and the other outstations, but, after a fortnight's investigation including a confrontation with the East German young lady in Berlin, I was able to give our 'John Smith' a clean bill of health.

CHAPTER 8

I WAS UNAWARE at the time that these various aggressive activities were taking place against the Soviet Union and satellite countries. So there was some initial surprise when I was given my new assignment, which was to be the MI6 liaison officer with the Royal Navy in Hamburg, in an operation which involved the covert transporting and landing of agents on the Latvian coast.

By 'aggressive', I mean that we were actually getting up and doing something, the attendant risks of which could all too easily cause a major diplomatic incident. In later years, it has always amazed me that these various operations were authorized by a Labour government in London, and I attributed this to the power of the Foreign Secretary, Ernest Bevin.

Part of my briefing covered the fact that the Germans, during the war, had used their very fast S-boats to carry agents on to the beaches of the Baltic States. We intended to recruit one of the most successful of the S-boat captains, Lieutenant Commander Hans Helmut Klose, to carry out similar operations for SIS using one of the S-boats. The S208, which had been built by Lurgens in Vegasack, was taken to a British yard near Portsmouth, stripped down and then souped up so that she would do almost fifty knots. The cover of the operation was that Klose, his German crew and the S208 were part of the British Control Commission Fishery Protection Service which operated in the Baltic to keep an eye on West German fishermen's rights. The East Germans had already set up a miniature navy with armed sea-going vessels as part of their border protection service. I was not involved in recruiting the Baltic agents who, in the main, were enlisted from Displaced Persons camps in Germany with the aid of émigré organizations with whom we were in contact.

Youngish men were recruited. Those who were, firstly, ideologically sound; secondly, who were prepared to return to their homelands and for whom a fitting cover story could be produced; and, thirdly, who could successfully complete our training course which involved instruction in radio, weapons, explosives and subjects essential to secret communications such as codes, cyphers and the use of secret inks.

After being recruited the agents were quietly flown to the UK for training and, about a week before they were due to set off, were returned to an RAF airfield in Germany accompanied by their conducting officer.

My job was to liaise with the naval intelligence officers involved in supervising Klose and his vessel, and to see that, from the time the agents arrived in Germany to the time they boarded the S208, they were securely housed and adequately protected. After they had boarded the S208 my job was to liaise with Naval Intelligence during the progress of the boat's mission, since she would keep radio silence until she had dropped our agents and was on her return voyage.

The first part of my new task meant meeting the Navy in Hamburg and during the time I was involved with them there were two flag officers, firstly Rear Admiral the MacKintosh of MacKintosh who was succeeded by Rear Admiral 'Shrimp' Simpson. I became an honorary member of the wardroom and much enjoyed pink gin at 2d a tot.

The senior officer with whom I had most to do was Commander Antony Courtney, a bluff seaman who later became a Member of Parliament. Having been set up by the KGB his career was ruined as the result of a staged bedroom indiscretion in a Moscow hotel, which the KGB photographed.

As my first job was to find a suitable house in Hamburg where the agents could live comfortably and safely for the few days between their arrival and the weather conditions being right for the operation, I contacted the local Control Commission Housing Officer who showed me the various requisitioned houses which were available. The set scale for this house was of the level that might be made available for a full colonel in the Army, and in due course I chose a beautiful old house with overgrown grounds running down to the Elbe in the Blankenese district of Hamburg. This building had the advantage of being approached along a private drive and was also secluded. It had a large and dusty loft area which we turned into a communication centre. This done, a team of wireless operators took over and set up their communication links with SIS Headquarters in London, SIS Headquarters in Germany and with the S208. The house was furnished by the Control Commission housing people, and we then seconded from the SIS corps of ancillaries a cook, kitchen and household staff.

On the appointed day for the arrival of the first group of agents I drove down to RAF Buckeberg to welcome them and their conducting officer, Peter. We used two 15-cwt Opel Blitz trucks with CCG numbers and an Opel saloon car. The agents came complete with their equipment, automatic weapons, ammunition, wireless sets and, not least, their money belts which carried a ransom in gold coins.

We had a normal and uneventful journey back to our safe house. My problem – which was a tricky one – was how to keep three agents entertained without risking their security and without allowing them an opportunity to brood on the danger of what they were soon to do.

We arranged an hour's physical training every morning and in the afternoon there was generally a siesta. Our evenings were generally filled playing chess, draughts or cards.

Peter and I debated whether it would be useful for the agents to have a trial run in the S208 and we agreed it would. We went down to a jetty on the Elbe one morning and the S208 drew alongside. Then we headed down the Elbe, gradually picking up speed but never doing more than about two-thirds of the possible revs. The agents were impressed with Klose and his crew's superb boat handling, and I decided that while we were taking what might be considered an unnecessary security risk, it was a calculated risk which was outweighed by the good it would do.

Not unnaturally, these young men were eager for some female company and I had solemn discussions with the local Control Commission Intelligence Officer to see if he could direct me towards some reliable prostitutes.

On the evening of the day we had the S208's trial run, I

arranged with Peter that he would take the three agents down to the Reeperbahn, the red light district of Hamburg. We all trooped off to a little bar which had in its favour an erotic floor show and a manager who was an informant of the local Field Security Section. We soon had the company of four over-madeup girls and some heavy drinking began, with our three young agents drinking nikolaschkas; thimble glasses of German brandy with sugar and powdered ginger poured on to a slice of lemon balanced on the top of the glass. The whole lot was to be drunk back in one. The evening progressed and, as I had a lot to do, I left the agents in Peter's company and went back to the house in Harvesterderhuderweg where I was staying – only a stone's throw from the safe house where our Baltic agents were billeted.

At about three in the morning I heard violent banging on my front door and found one of the radio operators standing outside asking me to come over to the safe house immediately. Two of our agents had returned by themselves. Peter and the other agent had got into a fight with some other customers in the bar. Luckily the other two had felt it wisest to slip out and had taken a taxi back to Blankenese. They had not known the exact address but fortune had been with them and they had recognized the overgrown drive leading down to the house.

This irresponsible performance could have led to the cancellation of the operation if the trouble concerning Peter and the third 'joe' resulted in any publicity or blowing of cover.

My immediate task was to get hold of the Control Commission Intelligence Division's Duty Officer and I arranged to meet him at the nightclub. When we arrived it was obvious that there had been some serious fighting, and the manager told us regretfully that he had been unable to do anything except call the police. They had taken away our two miscreants, along with several other of the people involved in the fight. The Intelligence Division officer and I hurried down to the police station and my companion, through his long-standing contacts with the local police, was able to get Peter and the Latvian released into our custody.

The shock of arrest had sobered them up so that when we got them back to the safe house we were able to go immediately into a post-mortem. From my point of view, the essential thing I needed to know was whether anybody involved in the evening's fight had been able to determine that these two were involved in an intelligence mission, and, if so, how much had anyone been able to glean. After a couple of hours of going endlessly over every aspect of the evening's events I was satisfied that neither the young tarts nor any of the other people in the bar would have learnt anything more than that Peter was a drunken English businessman, with a friend who was obviously not English but who was a business colleague.

In later years, after the Kim Philby and George Blake episodes, I began to wonder how many times they had committed similar slips which, if reported by a colleague, might have put the Service on its guard.

It was clear to me that if I reported Peter he would either be dismissed or else suffer a severe setback in the Service. I therefore decided to do nothing about it, and hushed up the whole matter. I noticed, however, that the two agents who returned home on their own had a more reserved attitude towards Peter than previously.

Our intended departure next morning in the S208 was delayed for twenty-four hours by bad weather. The wait following on from the fiasco of a fight brought about a certain tension in the safe house and I was relieved the next night when the Navy and Klose confirmed that the operation was on.

We went down to the jetty at about 4 p.m. and loaded all the kit and equipment aboard, and I bade farewell to the party. Peter and I then watched as the S208 slid out towards open water, and then we returned to our safe house to listen for radio signals from the S208. From half distance to the Latvian coast they were to keep radio silence, and on their return only send a short success signal when they were well away from the Soviet-controlled coasts.

However, that night it was not to be and I got a signal that bad weather and a failure of the navigational gear was forcing the S208 to return. I later sent my own signal to the Chief Controller of Europe, Kenneth Cohen, in Head Office in London asking that our Chief 'bang the table' in the Admiralty about the failings of navigational equipment which Klose had reported to me.

Klose and his men decided to take advantage of what the

forecasters promised would be a calm patch and next night they completed a successful operation. In due course our agents came on air with their first contact.

Many years later I heard through a friend in intelligence that all the agents dropped by the S208 and, later, by a second S-boat were picked up by the KGB and our wireless sets were played back at us. Like most security lapses, this one has been laid at Kim Philby's door. It is only recently, having had access to a television film made by East German television, that a different possibility has entered my mind. The film *Rotten Knechte* re-enacts the whole of the S208 operation with East German actors taking the part of Klose, the agents and me.

The re-enactment, however, is not devoted to just one operation. We are told that later on no warning was given to the groups already landed, or to the resistance movement in Latvia about later landings, although the whole set-up was now Russian controlled. In the film we see the S208 edging its way into the beach on the other side of the Latvian coast, supposedly with nobody aware that she is coming, and then suddenly we are shown a Soviet reception committee waiting for the boat's arrival.

I am quite sure that, while Kim Philby at his liaison post in Washington was privy to the general outline of our S208 operations, he would not have had detailed latitude and longitude positions for this landing, nor would he have had the exact timing. This therefore could point a finger at somebody else close to the operation, possibly even within SIS or in the Navy.

With the completion of this phase of our operation I returned to Headquarters and worked as a staff officer on various assignments. For two months I combed various Displaced Persons camps in the British zone of Germany, looking for likely agents prepared to return to their own countries, and collecting any Eastern bloc documents which our Forgery Section could use.

I was happy to be called off this rather mundane work by Derek and told that I was being posted to Berlin to take over the war planning activity in that station.

In the event of Germany being overrun by war with the

Russians, caches of wireless sets, explosives and arms and ammunition were stashed all over Germany; both in the Soviet and the British zones, and in Berlin. Our agents in East Germany took their stores back piecemeal and these were then carefully hidden, generally underground but often in houses, barns or the other sort of places found secure by various resistance movements during the Second World War.

Our first priority was to cache a number of wireless sets and codes. I decided that the most satisfactory place for some of these to be hidden was in the Grunewald. Our cover for this should be military, I thought, since the Army unit stationed in Berlin used the Grunewald for training exercises.

I appeared this time in the guise of a Royal Engineer Officer, and Sidney, who was a wireless specialist helping me in this work – and the W/T trainer for our agents – appeared as a Royal Signals Officer.

We got the local Army workshops to fix up a jeep for us with RE markings, and to fit to it a large detachable spotlight with about twenty metres of cable. Dressed in civilian clothing, we reconnoitred the general area during the daytime, using as our excuse either a picnic or a birdwatching expedition, depending on the weather. When we located a suitable site we drew its position on a large-scale map, adding the sort of directions that would have done justice to *Treasure Island*. Four paces north of this oak, two paces west from large twin-pointed boulder, and so on.

One problem that worried me was that the wireless sets, sealed in their cases, which were supposed to be weatherproof and safe for at least three years from any chemical reaction as a result of being buried, were heavy and the earth in which we were going to bury them was extremely moist. The boxes were fairly small with two making up a kit, so I designed a wooden box made from one inch board with a lip around the top of about four inches on each side, which I hoped would prevent the package sinking and would also keep the two units together.

Our task was to dig a hole about three feet deep in which to bury the box, itself about a foot high. We dug this under the cover of a military night exercise, hence our military vehicle and uniforms. It seemed likely the only people we might be seen by were courting German couples using the woods for their nocturnal pleasures, or German police, who had no authority to question us but would summon the Military Police if they felt we were up to something.

We cached four lots of equipment in this way and on only one occasion were we stopped by Military Police while returning from a dig. Rather than flashing our intelligence documents, we told them that we were on a night exercise and if they had any doubts they should ask the Assistant Provost Marshal to speak to the GOC's Military Assistant (whom we made sure to brief as soon as he arrived at his desk next morning).

Our social life was very gay in Berlin. I was delighted to discover that Claude Dewhurst, of the magnificent Mercedes and whom I had first met in Cairo, was now in Berlin as a brigadier commanding Brixmis. He gave magnificent parties which, from time to time, got more than a little out of hand. Indeed Claude called me one morning to warn me that one of his guests, who had been dancing in Claude's fountain at a party, had had a photograph taken in a compromising position with a young German boy. Claude's friend – who was of use to us – was anxious that the photographs should be retrieved before they damaged his civilian career. I promised that I would do what I could and a bit of quick action on the part of one of our agents soon brought the poor man relief and us a fair measure of gratitude.

In retrospect, there were a substantial number of homosexuals at work in intelligence in Germany. At the time my own pursuit of young women kept me from being over-interested in my colleagues' pleasures but, even so, it came as a bit of a shock when two of my colleagues – one a lieutenant colonel and the other a major – suddenly disappeared; one to prison and the other out of the Service for being caught *in flagrante* with young German boys. In their case the situation was so bad as to preclude any hushing up of the matter.

CHAPTER 9

'TONY, GET OVER HERE.'

The weekend of 25 to 27 May 1951 proved to be a memorable one. May is always a beautiful time of the year in Berlin, and in those days West Berliners, though surrounded by the Soviet zone, often took picnics to the Grunewald and the Waansee to enjoy the perfections of nature which even Russian occupation could not spoil. The brief telephone call to my flat near the Blue and White tennis club summoned me to the Olympic Stadium; which was not only British military headquarters but also the main office of SIS. I arrived and was surprised to find that all the officers of the station were assembling. But then our Station Commander began handing out photographs of two men. They were, he explained, two British diplomats, Donald McLean and Guy Burgess who, it was believed, intended to defect and might well pass through Berlin.

Each of us was detailed to watch a specific crossing point to see if we could recognize them. I do not recall that we were instructed to stop them but, in any event, after forty-eight hours and a sleepless weekend, we were all called off and learnt in due course that the two had defected without coming anywhere near Berlin.

Early in June I received a message from my Station Commander that I was to travel from Berlin down to the British zone as Big John wanted to see me. I decided to drive down the autobahn – which the occupying powers were allowed to do – and I remember the journey well because I used our 'military' jeep for the trip. A short way out of Berlin I came to the first Soviet checkpoint, where I was stopped by a rather young, sullen Red Army sentry with rifle and fixed bayonet and a sergeant with a machine pistol. The sergeant carefully read my inter-zonal pass and waved me through. Then I drove down the autobahn towards Helmstedt, at the statutory fifty miles an hour, noting mentally the large number of Red Army vehicles going about their duties, most of them carrying armed troops. At Helmstedt another, more cursory check and I drove on into the British zone and down towards Herford.

Next morning I reported to John's office and had to wait. When he arrived he asked me gruffly to sit down. He was sorry, he said, but he had some bad news. London had received a confidential report written on me after my first three years in the Service and had decided on the basis of the report that I was not suitable to be confirmed as a 'long-term' SIS officer.

This was a bitter blow.

I immediately protested and John said that my report had been compiled by Derek, who had written that he was unable to make up his mind about me and thus felt that, if he could not himself be certain about my suitability, it would be wrong to give me the benefit of the doubt.

Had I known then what I know now I would have played my hand very differently. Some years after I eventually left the Service I was informed by a serving member that Derek had been a former member of the Communist Party, had lied during his vetting procedure and about whom the truth was only later discovered during an intensive shake-up of SIS that happened when Sir Dick White took over as Chief. Derek was then sacked but this did not undo what he had already done to me.

I left Germany bitter but determined to fight the decision. It was probably as well that Maurice was in the Far East or, upset as I was, I might well have embarrassed him by asking him for friendship's sake to fight my battle.

Taking my courage in my hands, I demanded to see Commander Kenneth Cohen, the Chief Controller for Europe and the man, under the Chief, directly responsible for activities in the whole of Europe. I decided that this was not a time for modesty and gave him a summary of my achievements, emphasizing not only that I was an outstanding linguist but also that what seemed mostly to be held against me was that I was still considerably younger than anybody else that I worked with. Cohen told me to go away and come back and see him twenty-four hours later. When I did so, he announced that he was revoking the decision made on the basis of

Derek's report, that I would be posted to Vienna and the future was up to me. The Controller under Cohen responsible for Austria was called Philip, and I had to report to him for my instructions. (Again, it is only in recent years that I have discovered that Philip too was a one-time member of the Communist Party.)

There were similarities between the Berlin station and the Vienna station, since both cities were then occupied by the four powers even though well behind the Iron Curtain. But the SIS operation in Germany was large and supported by occupation costs, while the operation in Vienna was small and based at the British Embassy.

I had already had a serious fight with the Station Commander in Vienna during my time in R5, over one of his pet agents known as 'Dandelion'. This agent having been fairly successful for us as a double agent had suddenly announced that his Russian case officer was pushing him to move to South America. If we wanted him to go this would involve the Service providing him with a new passport and also a considerable amount of money.

Both my colleague in R5 dealing with South America and I were convinced that Dandelion was a fraud, who was using us to pay for his resettlement plans. We opposed the project and it went up to ACSS[1] Air Commodore Jack Easton for a decision. He overruled us and supported the Station Commander.

It was therefore somewhat gratifying, in a bizarre way, that a few months later, after Dandelion had arrived in Venezuela, he gave the station two fingers and the Vienna Station Commander reluctantly had to accept that we had been tricked. I had been right but that did not endear me to the Vienna station.

Since I was to take the Service car supplied to me up to Vienna, I planned a week's trip that would take me through Cologne, Munich and Salzburg, and then on to Vienna.

I felt that I wanted to thumb my nose at Derek so I arranged my route to take me past the German station and stopped off to spend a night there with them. Derek quickly told me how delighted he was that I was still in the Service, and had he only known how London would react to his report he would have worded it in an entirely different manner. Privately I doubted this.

[1] Assistant Chief Secret Service.

I had not been briefed on my cover before leaving for Vienna but had assumed I would be in the Embassy, although I knew there was currently no diplomatic slot available. In the event, I was told I was to be in Int. Org., the intelligence organization of the Austrian Control Commission. The Embassy had an Embassy Liaison Officer to Int. Org. and, for cover purposes, I was to be the Int. Org. Liaison Officer with the Embassy. My office, therefore, was in Schoenebrun Barracks and a new SIS secretary for me was posted out from London with Int. Org. cover.

My main assignment was to establish a war plan system as I had done in Berlin and to run two agents, one who supplied information on the Soviet Army and Air Force and one who supplied us with economic information, mainly on Austrian oil production and its shipment to the East.

I took rooms in the Park Hotel in Schoenebrun, which, at that time, was requisitioned for use by British officers. My accommodation was extremely comfortable and my stay there started a love affair which still continues with the Wiener Schnitzel. I would order a Wiener Schnitzel at the drop of a hat, particularly relishing them when put in brown Austrian peasant bread as a makeshift sandwich. My friends point to my time in Vienna as the beginning of my corpulent build-up!

The Station Commander in Vienna and I did not instantly take to each other, but that did not worry me since he was at the end of his tour and was shortly to be replaced. My colleagues numbered four at the Embassy and another two with me under Control Commission or military cover. Luckily, the officer I dealt with most at the Embassy was a woman, a former ATS officer who was our expert on Soviet forces. What did surprise me was that some of them appeared to me to be homosexuals. I have since discovered that most homosexuals in the Service are almost invariably prima donnas in their attitude to their work.

While I was not particularly close to the Station Commander who was about to leave, I was made no happier by the news that he was to be replaced by Philip from London; the former Communist who gave the impression of being homosexual as well. The two agents I had to run had already been recruited, and it was therefore only a question of them being handed over to me, but the stay-behind network I was to manage had to be set up from scratch.

By its very nature, and the fact that a stay-behind network has to remain asleep until needed, stay-behind agents cannot be recruited through agents with whom one is already in contact. The reason is obvious. If a current agent were caught he or she could blow part of the stay-behind network if the network had been based on an agent recruited through him.

My immediate task was the control of my two active agents; Hans, an Austrian, had been an officer in the German army and consequently had a mastery of things military, while Edgar, a Doctor of Economics, worked in the main office of the Austrian oil company on the other side of the Danube at Zistersdorf. Hans was about thirty-five, blond, blue-eyed and a great, though almost obsessive, athlete. He strode around in leather knickerbockers, heavy walking shoes and a thick white pullover; summer and winter, morning and evening. At that time, apart from the usual troop-watching activities (which to a large extent consisted of taking down and identifying vehicle numbers), our priority was to get clear photographs of the Russian MIG fighter plane.

Head Office had developed an automatic robot camera with a sight through the lens which enabled agents to pan the camera on an aeroplane in flight, even when the camera was equipped with a 175mm telephoto lens. Of course, when these aircraft flew over Vienna, they were always so high that even a good telephoto lens could not give a satisfactory picture. The trick, therefore, was to take the photographs near a Russian airfield, and one of the main ones was at Wiener Neustadt, about forty miles south of Vienna on the way to Graz and Klagenfurt. It was understandably dangerous to be caught loitering near a Soviet airfield, and to do so would be perilous with the type of camera we were using.

Hans tried first. He used to set off with a rucksack, on foot as though enjoying the wildlife. Unfortunately, although he knew various hides in which to wait close to the airfield at Tulln, we were not getting good enough pictures. After a while, when we were still not getting the pictures we needed, I decided to try for some myself.

Members of the British Occupational Forces in Vienna were

allowed to leave Vienna by the road to the Semmering, provided they were in possession of a grey pass. Grey passes had to be signed by the Soviet Kommandetura and it obviously drew suspicion if one person kept going up and down without good reason.

I have always been interested in fishing and just over the Semmering Pass, and in what was the British zone, the river Murz is close to a small village called Kindberg. There was a superb pub and guest house at Kindberg and since the military were given Wednesday afternoons off for recreation, I took to spending Wednesday afternoons, Saturdays and sometimes Sundays at Kindberg ostensibly for the purpose of fishing. I had the special camera with me. Whenever I saw any MIGs I would lift the bonnet of my car and then peer under it, but in such a way that I could hold the camera and focus it for the shot I wanted, and photograph whatever MIGs were in sight. I eventually got so daring (or reckless) that I began pulling up as close to the airfield as I could and photographing MIGs on the ground; although some time during this activity the Russians took to building blast shelters for the jets until all I could see of them were the tips of the tails.

In Melk I discovered a nice little beer shop with seats on its terrace where Soviet officers gathered. Melk, the site of an early Benedictine Abbey whose situation compared with that of Monte Casino, was not far from St Poelten, which was the Headquarters of the Soviet army in Austria. Thus my interest in church architecture developed quickly, just as my interest in fishing waned, and most weeks I would apply for a grey pass to travel into the Soviet zone to visit the abbey at Melk. After a cursory visit to the abbey I would sit myself on the terrace of the little pub and, whenever Soviet officers appeared, would seek to get into conversation with them if it could be done unobtrusively. I always used German. Sometimes it was obvious that they were suspicious and did not wish to talk, but eventually a young Russian Artillery Captain struck up conversation with me which, in due course, led to him proposing a drinking competition.

Draught beer was served in various sizes of glass at the pub, including a vast glass holding two litres which was called a *Stiefel*, a riding boot. The glass was made in that shape and in that size.

My new Russian friend challenged me to drink a *Stiefel* of beer and a glass of vodka if he would do the same. Then we would repeat the process until the one who gave up first was the loser. I imagine the Russian officer had had a bad night or had been out on the town the evening before because, as our contest continued he had to leave the table and rush to the lavatory. He looked rather green on his return and we both decided the contest was over.

Tactfully, I did not insist I had won but said rather that ill health caused us to call it off. I added we should try again on another occasion, at which my Russian friend told me that he normally came into Melk if not on duty and said he thought he would be in again the Sunday after next. I could not make any preparation for my next meeting with him as I did not know his name, only his first name and patronymic which were Grigori Vassilevitch, and those were not sufficient to see if there was any trace of him in SIS records.

A fortnight later I returned to Melk and was slightly surprised to see that Grigori was already there, sitting in the pub drinking a beer. He was on his own. I assumed, since it was a beautiful day, that the reason he was sitting inside and by himself was because he was meeting me.

This was dangerous. Either it meant he was out to entrap me or it meant that he wanted to talk to me knowing me to be British, with the British Commission and therefore, to the suspicious mind of a Soviet officer, possibly a spy.

I drew up a chair and ordered a beer, a small one. Grigori told me he wanted to apologize for his behaviour the previous time we had met. Something he had eaten the evening before had not agreed with him and this accounted for his impolite behaviour. I commiserated, in a fully-understanding manner, and said we had been silly to drink so much even though it was obvious that we were both good drinkers. At this we clinked glasses.

From then on I carried on a conversation discussing everything and anything except matters to do with the Soviet forces or his work. We talked about our families, home life, what we had done as children, what brothers and sisters we had, what our parents did, and so on. In order to ingratiate myself I told him that my father had been a factory worker, who had been unemployed for a long time, and after he had died I had been brought up by my mother. He told me that his father had been killed in the war by the Germans and that he, himself, had been in the Red Army for the famous advance on Berlin, and that he planned to stay in the army. He was now a captain in the Artillery with an office job in St Poelten, the Soviet Military Headquarters.

I said immediately that, in this case, it might be difficult for him if he were seen talking to a foreigner for too long, but he dismissed this saying that he knew what he could and could not do.

The obvious thought to me was that if I could continue and build on my acquaintanceship with Grigori I might, at some later time, be able to recruit him as a source – a Staff Officer from Soviet Military Headquarters in Austria would be worth his weight in gold.

I introduced myself using a pseudonym, I think it was probably Paul Carpenter at this time. He told me his name. Hoping I was on my way to something big as we bade each other farewell, I returned to Vienna to plan my next move.

We had agreed to meet again a fortnight later, same place, same time. I arrived as arranged but there was no sign of Grigori, and though I waited as long as I dared he did not arrive. I waited until early evening and then set off back to Vienna feeling rather depressed. A fortnight later I went to the pub again and this time saw three Soviet officers drinking on the terrace. I had seen two of them previously as part of the group when I first saw Grigori. I sat down and ordered a drink, waiting to see if they would say anything to me. When they did not, I was faced with deciding whether to risk approaching the officers myself to ask after Grigori, or else finding another way.

The first was too risky, so I went into the pub to the kitchen and explained to the proprietor, who knew me now from my several visits, that I was anxious to enquire after Grigori but for various reasons did not want to approach the Russians myself. I asked him politely if he would mind enquiring after Grigori, saying that the last time Grigori had been he had left behind a box of cigarettes, which fortunately the landlord had picked up.

Some other Russian visitor had left his cigarettes behind and I had pocketed them. I gave them to the landlord and waited inside while the landlord performed his charade. He came back shortly telling me that one of the Russians, who had been rather angry at the question, had told him that Captain Grigori would not be coming for his cigarettes because he had been posted back to the Soviet Union.

The fact that the Russians gave this information indicated that alcohol was already loosening their tongues, but what was even more clear was that any plans we had to recruit Grigori were over. He was the first of three Russian officers whose acquaintance I made and who then disappeared.

My second Soviet contact came as a result of a visit to the opera. During a break in a performance of *Boris Godounov,* with George London singing the main part, I went for a drink in the bar. As I stood at the bar alone I found in fact that I was standing close to a Russian Army Colonel whose shoulderboards told me he was in the Artillery. It was easy, when he turned around glass in hand, to ensure that in doing so he made me spill some of my drink. He apologized immediately and insisted with a smile on buying me a fresh drink.

'I would be delighted,' I replied, but only on condition that I could reciprocate. He hesitated and when the bell rang for an end to the interval he agreed to meet for the second interval at the same spot.

Naturally, my thoughts were not with the opera for the next fifty minutes or so. I was excited and expectant when I moved back to the bar for my second encounter with the Colonel. He arrived as agreed and I ordered our drinks. We began by talking about the opera and moved on to exchanging personal details. He was on the staff at Soviet Headquarters in Vienna, which were in the Imperial Hotel a short way down the Ring from the Opera House.

I told him in return that I was in the Control Commission. He did not enquire further as to what my job was, though mentally I had determined that I would tell him I was an historian if asked.

His friendliness and openness were such that I felt safe in asking him to have lunch with me. He accepted readily enough and we arranged to meet in the basement brasserie of a local brewery, the Goesserbrau, three days later.

Next morning I discussed the whole matter in detail with Philip who decided that London's guidance should be sought. Unfortunately, it being a first meeting, I had only got the first name of my colonel and we were therefore unable to pass his full name through our records to see if we already had trace of him.

A signal sped back from London authorizing me to continue the contact, and Philip said that I would be kept under observation while with Nikolai. The fact that we were meeting in a dimly lit restaurant meant that concealed photography would be difficult.

I was impatient for the day of the lunch to arrive. The thought that we might be at the start of an enterprise which, if handled well, could land us a defector from Soviet Headquarters in Vienna was exciting for everybody.

I arrived at the Goesserbrau about ten minutes before the appointed time and chose a table between two others that were unoccupied. The tables with benches were set in the centre of three-sided stalls and, in the normal Austrian tradition, if the place got full, strangers could ask if they might take a spare place at a table.

Nikolai arrived punctually at 12 o'clock and joined in a beer and also ordered himself an iced schnapps to go with it. We tucked into the special dish of the day, which was boiled beef and dumplings, and as we ate we discussed Vienna, occupied Austria, the world situation and then the war. Nikolai was an intelligent man, with some personal knowledge of life outside occupied territory since he had visited France with some kind of Soviet military mission. Towards the end of the meal he told me his full name, and it was easy to remember because his last name was the same as the well-known General of Polish origin, Rokossowski.

We had a longish meal and shortly after 2 o'clock he said he must return to his office. I took care to pay for the lunch at which he asked if I would join him the following week for a meal as his guest.

I accepted as casually as I knew how, and he mentioned that he knew a very good little restaurant called the Bulgar, off the Graben in the centre of Vienna. We agreed to meet there, just before eight in the evening in a week's time.

Now that we knew Nikolai's full name we were able to pass him through our records and confirm that he was indeed a Staff Officer in the Soviet Commander-in-Chief's secretariat. He was thus an extremely valuable contact, either as a potential defector or, better still, as a potential source.

However, a complication now arose. In naming that particular restaurant the Russian Colonel had given us a problem. The Bulgar was in the international sector of Vienna, where the Soviets had as much right to operate as any of the other occupying powers. It would not therefore be very difficult for them to arrange to kidnap me on a pretext of first arresting me, in company with the Austrian police, based on a complaint lodged by my Soviet friend. For, if he was in touch with Soviet intelligence or indeed was himself a KGB officer, he could be playing exactly the same game as I was. It was decided, therefore, that we would have to stake out the restaurant so that help would be at hand in the event of anything untoward happening.

I arrived in the restaurant at about ten past eight, giving Nikolai – as host – the chance to get there first. After half an hour we started to get worried and decided after an hour that he was not coming. We assumed either that something had come up which prevented him from keeping the dinner date, or that he had mentioned meeting me to a colleague and that the KGB had forbidden him to attend.

We had given each other a private telephone number on which we could be reached. So the next morning I arranged for a colleague, an émigré whose Russian was perfect, to ring the number and ask for Colonel Nikolai. My émigré friend called me later to say that when the telephone was eventually answered a brusque voice announced that Colonel Nikolai had recently returned to the Soviet Union.

I became friendly with my third Russian officer in Paris, but that was at a later date.

Before I had arrived in Austria, a Soviet military intelligence lieutenant had defected and had been spirited by us out of Austria.

This young officer had indicated his willingness to return to Vienna, provided he was suitably disguised, to help us identify Soviet intelligence officers active in the Austrian capital. I was elected to be his minder and case officer.

He flew in to Schwechat in a BEA plane accompanied by an officer from London. I met the defector and found a tall auburn-haired man of about twenty-eight with a fiery auburn moustache. I was later told that he was originally fair-haired and clean shaven and the colouring and moustache were the main part of his physical disguise.

I had arranged that 'Romanov', which was his code name, would live as a paying guest with a British major and his wife, who had a large flat and no children.

We had already acquired the use of a room in the offices of a British company then based directly opposite the Soviet Headquarters at the Imperial Hotel, and we sat up there with a camera which we used to take pictures of all Soviet officers going in and out of the Imperial. It was Romanov's job to sit in this room and name those officers he could, particularly letting us know those who were in Soviet intelligence. We achieved a lot through this operation – which gave us information we did not already possess and which lasted for almost a month. I then bade farewell to my young friend and he left Vienna for I know not where.

One of the most successful British operations ever was carried out at this time in Vienna. SIS agents dug a long tunnel from a house in the British sector through to where they could tap into the telephone lines from Russian Headquarters in Vienna to Red Army Headquarters in St Poelten, and from St Poelten Head-quarters to Moscow. These intercepts were of enormous value, since they enabled an assessment to be made in London of any preparations which might indicate that the Soviets intended a military solution for the Cold War.

The whole Soviet order of battle, down to the whereabouts of this or that field bakery, was soon known to our Defence Intelligence Staffs.

In any event, the operation carried on successfully until a tram, passing over the tunnel where it went under a road, suddenly caused the tunnel to collapse and the tram to sink into the resulting deep depression. The whole matter was hushed up but that was the end of the operation. Of course, it was this operation in Vienna which inspired the similar – and more famous – one in Berlin.

Our success at tapping Soviet telephone wires gave me the idea for a further possibility. Many of the Soviet army lines to which we wanted to listen were in overhead wires. I came up with the idea of designing a farm cart, loaded with hay inside which would be a box (suitably ventilated), large enough to hold a man and recording equipment. This cart with the normal pair of horses would be drawn along the road and the top of the hay would be about a foot below the overhead telephone wires. When the farmer leading the horses gave the all-clear, the operator inside the cart should push up a needle-thin antenna to contact the wires and allow him to draw off the signals traffic.

The idea was considered interesting enough to research, so it became my job to find a suitable farmer, which I was able to do.

Meanwhile, my main duty was still to arrange caches of supplies for stay-behind people in the Russian zone in Lower Austria. Our main question, having recruited the right sort of agent, was how to transport the material. Obviously a light truck would be best, but if stopped at a Russian checkpoint it was easy for the guards to throw up the tarpaulin cover at the rear to look into it, which was hopeless. So as there were a number of large American cars in Austria, we decided to purchase one of these and have a false boot fitted within the enormous boot that American cars then had. I acquired a second-hand Chevrolet at a knock-down price from a departing American serviceman, and then had it registered as an Austrian vehicle with Austrian number plates.

I recruited the impecunious owner of a small garage and workshop and took the car to him, explaining that we wanted a secret compartment fitted behind the boot. When finished the compartment was approximately three and a half by one and a half by one and a half feet, so the car had to make three or four journeys for each cache.

I used the car to carry our secret supplies, surviving the various checkpoints. And in due course the dummy boot was removed, the car returned to its 'pristine' state and we even sold it for a profit in the used-car market!

I did a great deal of travelling by car when I was in Austria, either down the American route to the Enns Bridge, Linz and Salzburg or down the British route over the Semmering to Graz and Klagenfurt.

For about a month I also went regularly to Mariazell, where a Soviet private soldier had turned up seeking asylum, and we thought it possible some of his pals might like to join him.

One evening I was invited to dine with the GOC, General West. Another guest was the British High Commissioner Sir Harold (later Lord) Caccia. I was told afterwards by our Station Commander that the two of them had an argument about me, as each thought I worked for the other, and my Station Commander had to explain that I worked for neither since I was an SIS officer. My cover obviously needed improving!

My social activities at this time were devoted mainly to two of the young women working for the CIA, and I have to admit that coping with both of them at the same time diverted some of the energy that I should have been putting into intelligence. A colleague of mine had also suffered the same problem and had been admonished by George K. Young, an earlier Head of the Vienna Station who rose to be Deputy Chief of MI6, with the words, 'John, I don't give a damn what you do in your own time. As far as I'm concerned you can keep earwigs up your arse. Just don't let it interfere with your work.'

My relationship with our Station Commander, Philip, was also not of the best. I felt no great affection for him, largely because of his peccadilloes but also because of an unhouse-trained little Pekinese which he took around with him. His second-in-command was a naturalized Briton who could not have been more the opposite of Philip. I suppose I should have thought more about the fact that these two would be writing my next confidential report, but since I was doing a good job I felt I was entitled to what social relaxation was available.

Then coming back from a party in the American sector late one night I skidded in the spring slush and knocked a cyclist off his bike. Philip, with whom I had increasingly quarrelled, decided that this irresponsibility was not acceptable and wrote a stinging report which caused my recall to London.

There had been some changes in London since I was last there and the former Head of the Intelligence Division in Germany, General Charles Haydon, was now in SIS Headquarters as Director of Finance and Administration, and consequently Senior Personnel Officer. I was told by one of his deputies, whom I had known in Germany as one of my more pompous colleagues, that my career in SIS had come to an end.

I had no intention of accepting this without a fight and therefore demanded to see General Haydon. But both the personnel officer and the General were not of a type who really understood much about intelligence work in the field, and both felt that problems with personnel should be handled in the same way as in the Army.

So I was out. My career in SIS had been brought to an end by two former members of the Communist Party. It might have been the end of my career, but as events proved it was not to be the end of my associations.

Today I reflect that it was an odd situation, for when Maurice Oldfield became Chief he described me in a letter to the author Graham Greene as 'the cleverest young officer I ever recruited', and George Young who became Vice Chief of the Service described me recently in a newspaper as 'a first-class officer'.

CHAPTER 10

As INTELLIGENCE OPERATIVES cannot go around proclaiming who or what they are, they are invariably obliged to have 'cover'. Before the last war most British intelligence operations in foreign countries were grouped around the passport control officer in any consulate, who was responsible for the issue of visas. Very often the PCO was not only the MI6 representative but actually did all the work of his cover job.

Since the war this particular cover, which was always known to anybody who was interested, has been abandoned, and where MI6 officers now work in an embassy they generally do so as first, second and third secretaries, or else as attachés. One or two of the senior posts, such as the MI6 liaison officer in Washington, rank as a counsellor, and in some Third World countries, for example, the Consul General has also been an MI6 officer.

At the end of the war a number of MI6 agents were sent abroad under the cover of newspaper men. Indeed the Kemsley Press allowed many of their foreign correspondents to cooperate with MI6 and even took on MI6 operatives as foreign correspondents. However, this practice stopped when Kemsley's disappeared.

Other covers often used are as travelling businessmen or as local representatives of British business houses or semi-official organizations. In any event, hostile foreign intelligence services still treat most Britons or Americans residing in their countries as capable of being engaged in intelligence or espionage and watch them accordingly.

The type of people that MI6 recruit are, generally speaking, intelligent, middle class, ambitious and cultivated: so are their wives. Thus, as I said earlier, a wife's reaction on learning of her husband's posting overseas is often 'Are we to be in the Embassy?', followed by questions about the type of house on offer, the number of servants, the kind of car, whether there will be a chauffeur, and matters affecting the children's schooling. Whereas, lost behind the cloak of Soviet security, a senior or middle-ranking KGB officer can be posted abroad as a clerk, chauffeur or security guard to an embassy and will invariably leave his wife and children behind.

When a British SIS operative accepts a menial cover, the very fact that his children are away in England at boarding school reveals his status. So a private income must be invented.

Another habit of SIS which often causes confusion to the outsiders who work with SIS is that rank inside the Service does not necessarily compare with the importance of the job being done, or of the cover that is given.

The ranks of officer in SIS when I joined the Service went by six stages from Junior Officer to Director, and above the Directors came Assistant Chief, the Vice Chief and CSS himself. For comparison let us say that a junior officer was equal to something like a captain/major, a director to a brigadier, and the ranks in between counting as either senior majors, half colonels or colonels.

Officers who used military cover normally took on the rank that best suited them, but nearly everybody wanted to be at least a lieutenant colonel, and when I was in Germany, at least ten of the officers who used military cover were colonels. Having left the Army as a young captain, as soon as I was required to use military cover – when posted later on to Berlin – I reappeared as a major, with all the supporting documents signed where necessary by the GOC Berlin, at that time General Sir Geoffrey (later Lord) Bourne.

When I took up my first desk job in R5 with responsibility for the studying and penetration of Russian intelligence services in Germany, Austria and Switzerland – then probably one of the more important jobs in R5 – I was the most junior officer in the Service. Officers doing similar jobs were generally one rank and often two above me.

Thus, when two such senior officers as 'Gibby' and 'Perks' arrived in Germany there was speculation as to their assignment, given that in rank they were equivalent to Big John.

Another tell-tale factor about people's rank and their cover was the type of car with which they were issued, much like in commercial life. Most intelligence officers had Beetles, with a call on a pool Humber when necessary, but those officers who cared more for style than cover, and who had the rank to arrange it, drove large requisitioned American cars which immediately blew them to anyone who was interested.

Since the Russian mission in the British zone was head-quartered in our little town, no doubt this all made life easier for those of them engaged in watching us.

Chapman Pincher did us no service when he wrote in one of his books that merchant banking was used as a cover, and that SIS officers never lose contact with their organization when they retire. When I joined a merchant bank early in the 1970s, there were half a dozen ex-MI6 men working in the City of London. I know most of them and I am as sure as I can be that none of them is using his position as cover.

However, since I have been both a genuine journalist and merchant banker, it is often difficult to persuade people sufficiently knowledgeable about intelligence matters that such positions are not being used as cover.

The choice of cover used for Soviet operatives ranges right through all social scales. The heavy TIR (Transport International Routier) lorries that haul across Europe from the Channel ports to the Soviet Union and the Middle East make up an important part of the Red Army's intelligence-gathering machine. These lorries, sometimes with East German or satellite country number plates, often contain sophisticated electronic equipment and follow routes that intentionally take them close to defence installations and training areas.

Eastern bloc trucks may follow completely nonsensical routes, which force them to drive three to four times further than necessary, but which allow them to pass various military strong points. The blessing for the Soviets is that the entirely genuine TIR agreement guarantees the sealed goods compartments of trucks operating under this agreement free passage through customs of any of the signatory countries. Since this includes virtually all Western Europe and Soviet bloc countries, most of the trucks from the Iron Curtain have, at some time or another, carried Soviet tank or artillery commanders sent to obtain first-hand knowledge of the terrain over which they would advance in the event of war.

This lorry system is the means by which the Red Army intelligence maintains its order-of-battle charts, and this information also fills out that obtained by electronic means and by their interception of NATO signals.

Similarly, the Soviet Air Lines, headed by Aeroflot, make use of their commercial activities both on the ground and in the air to carry out spying missions. There are many who will always believe that the South Korean Boeing 747 shot down by the Russians in 1982 was a target because it strayed over Soviet territory close to secret defence installations while on a spying mission for American intelligence.

Soviet intelligence officers also staff tourist organizations in the Soviet Union and satellite countries. Intourist operatives accompany all tours to the Soviet Union made by foreigners, both to observe them and occasionally to earmark them for later recruitment. The manager or his deputy in an Intourist office in a Western capital is likely to be a KGB man. The same is true of the banks, particularly the Moscow Narody.

The tolerant attitude of immigration officers in the West to merchant seamen enables Soviet intelligence officers to move in and out of Western countries at will, using bogus merchant seamen's papers. Both the sailors on the high seas and those who sail up and down inland waterways such as the Danube have their sprinkling of intelligence men; as do trade fairs and exhibitions all over the world, which give the Russian intelligence agencies opportunities to apply for visas for their people who they can then describe as businessmen, technicians, scientists or factory managers.

Although bigger, better and more powerful computers have stepped up the amount spent from the budget on electronic intelligence by at least doubling the working capacity of computers, the number of solutions for every problem is squared, and overall results from SIGINT (Signals Intelligence) have deteriorated over the last few years and re-established HUMINT (Human Intelligence) – that is, field intelligence obtained by individuals on the ground. Thus the need for viable cover has once again become essential.

As in my own case, SIS officers operating in military areas take on military cover and, during the occupation of Austria and still even now in Germany, they use the cover of the overt intelligence organizations. In the colonial days, intelligence men appeared on the staff of the governor, and there was always a fall-back to the title of British adviser to this or that potentate.

In the end a good cover story can only be carried on by constant self-discipline and an acceptance that the job is more important than the person.

CHAPTER 11

I WAS OUT OF the Service now, and back in the same position in which I had found myself when I left the Army. I still felt that my best chance lay in a journalistic career. I was helped by George Young, who had previously been a journalist working for British United Press. He gave me an introduction to Frank Fisher who, during 1953, was the Managing Director of BUP. After a couple of interviews, Fisher introduced me to Roger Tatarian, General Manager of United Press of America (later United Press International), of which BUP was a British subsidiary. Tatarian controlled all the UP news gathering for Europe, the Middle East and Africa.

Tatarian decided he could make a newspaperman of me and took me on at £10 a week as a trainee. I had to learn to type and was used initially as a reporter and as an assistant to the European news editor. Tatarian was an excellent newspaperman, having long been the UP manager in Rome, and I owe my entire success in the journalistic field to him and his colleague, George Pipal, General Manager for Business, which meant selling the UP news services to clients in every country in Europe, the Middle East and Africa.

My real adventures in journalism started after I had been a trainee for a year, when I was considered ready to go out on my own. I was sent to Paris, where I rented a small three-roomed flat high above the river Seine on the Left Bank near Les Halles. Old Service habits die hard and I felt I should cultivate certain people in Paris. It is difficult for me now to remember the reasons why I eventually chose the Ambassadors of India, Poland and Yugoslavia as my targets, but choose them I did. The Indian was Wing Commander Sirdar Malik, the Pole was Stanislaw Gajewski and the Yugoslav was Alois Bebler. I also developed other friends, in particular the Tass correspondent, Ivan Saplin, who I knew to be a KGB Colonel.

Among French politicians, I got to know Pierre Mendes-France best, and spent two weeks with him during his 1956 election campaign. I also came to know Gaston Deferre, the Mayor of Marseilles and a future presidential candidate, and Pierre Poujade, the shopkeeper from St Cere who became the new right-wing leader supported by Jean Marie Le Pen, leader today of the right-wing faction in the French Parliament.

I had not been in Paris overlong before I was contacted by SIS.

I was approached by a secretary I had known while working for the Service in Germany, and she asked me to contact one of the Paris station officers, an émigré Pole and now naturalized British. It was the time of the XXth Party Congress in Moscow, when Nikita Khrushchev denounced Stalin and all his works. There was enormous pressure on Western agencies to come up with the complete text of Khrushchev's speech and SIS was pulling out every stop to try and get it. And that included asking me.

There were two possibilities as far as I was concerned: the Polish Ambassador or my Tass correspondent. I eventually got a copy from the Poles, but not before SIS managed to acquire one from a second source.

The life of a journalist in Paris at any time is exciting and my tour there was no exception. I was involved in covering Grace Kelly's romance and eventual marriage to Prince Rainier of Monaco in the splendour of Monte Carlo.

Paris was where I first met Randolph Churchill, whom I soon found to be a wonderful conversationalist, but who, if approached at the wrong moment or in the wrong way, could be insufferably rude.

The President of the United States sent Conrad Hilton, the hotel magnate, as his representative to Monte Carlo and Hilton invited me up to his suite for a drink. I found him a charming but wily old man, and wrote so in a piece about him which earned me a congratulatory letter from him. For a while after that we exchanged Christmas greetings.

I was also involved in covering another romantic interlude while based in Paris. I was shunted up to Brussels to keep track of Group Captain Peter Townsend during his doomed romance with Princess Margaret. I followed him to England and had the dubious distinction of being the first reporter to speak to him after the Princess had issued her statement saying that duty had forced her to end her relationship with him.

I asked Townsend how he felt.

He replied bleakly, 'It's all a closed book now.'

He was a charming man, courteous and brave, and many of us among the reporters tailing him felt more than a little ashamed.

I think it was one morning in January 1956 that I was sitting in the newsroom of our offices, one of the windows of which had a view of Eiffel's tower. One of our reporters, who was at the Prefecture on an enquiry, telephoned to announce that the Eiffel Tower was on fire.

'Pull the other one,' I said.

To which he rejoined, 'Look out of the window, you bloody fool!'

I did. It was. Smoke was pouring from the direction of the top of the tower. I rushed down to my car and drove to the tower at breakneck speed.

My *coupe fille* or press pass enabled me to get through the police cordons, and I found that all the lifts in the tower had been stopped. The only way to discover what was wrong was to climb the stairs. It was my bad luck to get sandwiched between two tough and fit young firemen who were also going up. Instead of going up at a leisurely pace, as I might have done, these two firemen set the pace, and a very fast pace it was. Climbing that must have taken me as near as I have ever been to having a heart attack.

It was some of the cables that had caused the fire, and the firemen soon had it under control. There were obviously no communications, so I then had to get down as quickly as I could to telephone in my story. I shall never forget the rapid climbing and descent of the Eiffel Tower.

Marshall Tito made a state visit to France during my time in Paris, and my affinity with the Ambassador ensured that I got as much background information as the Yugoslavs felt like giving. In addition, I was subsequently invited to Brioni, Tito's holiday island, to interview Tito, all of which stood me in good stead when I was later posted to Belgrade since I was able to call on one of the President's aides, Mirko Milotinovic. By that time, Bebler had become President of one of the Yugoslav states.

Being a bit too anxious to get a story during the Tito visit and getting myself in the wrong place at the right time, I came up against French security. I was roughed up by the French CRS – the Mobile Police – and led off by my tie, with a policeman each side of me, and thrown into a paddy-wagon and taken down to the police station. I was later released with apologies but it gave me a very healthy respect for the CRS.

One of the other friendships I made in the Indian Embassy was with Raja Dinesh Singh, a young diplomat who later became a figure in Indian politics and became a minister in Indira Gandhi's government. A colleague of his, whom I also got to know quite well, used to provide me with diplomatic petrol coupons. He also sought to involve me in various illegal currency transactions in which, thankfully, I did not indulge.

But perhaps the most charming man I had to deal with in Paris was Stanislaw Gajewski, the Polish Ambassador, an accomplished lawyer and a fine tennis player. We used to meet for a drink about once a month and my friendship with him was to pay enormous dividends.

In the summer of 1956 rioting broke out in Poznan in Poland and marked the beginning of unrest in the Soviet bloc which was to culminate in the Hungarian Revolution. United Press had a stringer in Warsaw but no regular correspondent, and the Polish authorities had clamped down on visas to Poland after the rioting since they were not about to welcome a horde of Western reporters at a time of unrest. One after another, United Press applied for various of their correspondents to go to Poland but all visa applications were rejected.

'Nothing ventured . . .' I thought, as I sent a message to London saying that I thought I might be able to get a Polish visa and asking should I try? When I had London's doubtful agreement I went to see Gajewski, who issued me with a visa immediately and without reference to Warsaw.

UP Headquarters in London were almost speechless, but since they urgently needed a correspondent in Warsaw, I was told to get there as quickly as I could. I flew first to Copenhagen and changed for a plane to Warsaw. UP's Warsaw stringer met me off the plane and took me to the Hotel Bristol, run by Orbis for foreign tourists and travellers. I immediately made the rounds of various ministries to build up contacts and got myself accredited at the Ministry of Foreign Affairs.

I was fortunate in that our stringer was already a drinking companion of the Prime Minister's press secretary and I immediately applied to the press secretary for an interview with the Prime Minister.

At this time the height of journalism where UPI was concerned was to obtain interviews with heads of government and heads of state. No foreign correspondent had yet been granted an interview with Prime Minister Jozef Cyrankiewicz, so it would obviously be a great coup for UPI if I could succeed where others had failed. Meanwhile, I filed several stories a day relating to the unsettled situation in Poland, all brought about by the revelations of points made in Khrushchev's XXth Congress speech.

At the end of July the press secretary confirmed that the Prime Minister intended to grant me an interview, which would also be televised, and I was to hold myself in readiness to be summoned to Cyrankiewicz's office.

Meanwhile, I made my number at the British Embassy where Sir Eric Berthoud was Ambassador, and I found that one of the senior diplomats on his staff was a former SIS colleague, who was then becoming notorious for carrying on a fairly public affair, much to the distress of his wife.

On 2 August I was told that my interview with the Prime Minister would be the following day, and on the 3rd I presented myself at the Prime Minister's office and was ushered in to meet one of the great leaders of the communist world.

Cyrankiewicz spoke German and a little English. He was obviously a civilized man, dressed in a well-cut suit, and in no way did he resemble the rather uncouth and carelessly-dressed Khrushchev. Cyrankiewicz was married to a well-known actress and had a certain European sophistication about him.

We agreed that I would ask him questions in English but that he would reply in Polish. My questions would then be dubbed for Polish television, while his answers would be dubbed for British and American television.

The interview went well and when it was over he asked me to have a drink with him. When I took my leave, he told his press secretary that, now I was an accredited correspondent in Poland, he should be advised of any time that I wished to see him.

Pleased as punch, I went back to my hotel room and prepared my story. The following day Polish radio started its early morning news bulletin by saying, 'The Polish press gave prominence today to the interview granted by the Chairman of the Council of Ministers Jozef Cyrankiewicz to United Press editor Anthony Cavendish.'

I hurried down to the lobby of the Bristol to get a copy of the Communist Party newspaper *Trybuna Ludu* and found most of the front page devoted to my interview, together with a good picture.

I had asked Cyrankiewicz how the events at Poznan would affect Polish life. He had assured me that they would have no repercussions on the continuing democratization of life in Poland, which, of course, quickly proved to be communist gobbledegook.

Often during the next few months people would say of the situation in Eastern Europe, 'The Hungarians have behaved like Poles, the Poles have behaved like Czechs and the Czechs have behaved like pigs.' The courageous Poles had shown their mettle at Poznan, but it was spontaneous and unprepared.

Over the next ten weeks there were stirrings of unrest throughout the communist empire. New newspapers appeared, such as *Monday News* in Budapest, which mocked People's democracies and helped a head of steam build up throughout August and September.

On 5 August I decided that, now I had a permanent visa for Poland and now that UP intended me to be their Eastern correspondent based in Warsaw, I should go back to Paris to clean up my flat and collect more clothes. I arrived back in Warsaw after a four-day drive through Czechoslovakia and a stopover in Prague at the end of a week of rumblings throughout Central Europe.

CHAPTER 12

ON TUESDAY, 23 OCTOBER the lid blew off. But it was the Hungarians who showed the way, not the Poles.

Word came to me first from London. The UPI day editor Danny Gilmore called me and asked for Polish reaction to what proved to be the beginning of the Hungarian uprising.

I asked if we had a staff man in Budapest.

'No, we do not,' Gilmore said.

I offered to go, but was told to stay where I was for the moment and cover Poland.

Eventually, three days after the Hungarian revolt began, UPI still did not have a reporter in Budapest as nobody had been able to get through, so I was told to get there if I could possibly manage it.

Basil Davidson of the *Daily Herald* had already told me he was going to get a lift to Budapest on a Polish Red Cross plane. So, on the evening of 27 October I presented myself at Warsaw airport and asked for the airport duty officer.

'Your Prime Minister's secretary tells me that a Red Cross plane is going to Budapest and that I should use it.'

The duty officer doubted what I was telling him – to put it mildly – so I presented him with a copy of *Trybuna Ludu*, complete with my interview and picture with Cyrankiewicz.

'Why don't you call the Prime Minister's residence?' I suggested.

My bluff worked. It was late, after midnight, and the duty officer agreed that I should go. Davidson looked surprised to find me on what he thought was his exclusive transport to the revolution, but soon he relaxed and proved very informative. Davidson was an MC from wartime services in SOE, and, as I soon learned, a very brave man.

Our plane was a C-47 Dakota carrying 2200 pounds of blood plasma. We flew low because of fog and rain and were unable to land at Budapest. Eventually, we touched down just after 5 a.m. at Kishkunlacheza, thirty-three miles south of the capital, passing squadrons of lined-up silver MIG-15 jet fighters, as we skimmed down the main runway. Both Basil Davidson and I congratulated our pilot Viktor Pekla. It was a difficult flight and a worse landing, but landing at all was an achievement.

I scrounged a ride into Budapest in a Polish legation car and then set to work. I still have a copy of the first despatch I sent out on 29 October to the free world, describing what I found in Hungary.

Soviet tanks and troops crunched out of this war-battered capital carrying their dead with them.

They left a wrecked city where the stench of death already rises from the smoking ruins to mingle with chill fog from the Danube river.

I arrived here from Warsaw by plane, car and foot, walking the last five miles into the bleeding heart of this once beautiful city.

As we approached the centre of Europe's worst upheaval since the last war I saw the full horror of devastation the revolution had brought.

No sooner were we on the road north to Budapest than we ran into a massive southbound Soviet convoy headed by two armoured cars.

Ten T-54 tanks, their red stars still visible through the grime of gunpowder, oil and blood, waddled behind, leaving Budapest.

Then came numerous motorcycles and trucks.

On the back of one tank lay the corpse of a Soviet soldier, his eyes staring vacantly back at the Hungarian capital. Other bodies were in the trucks. The Russian tankmen in their black crash helmets looked tired and grim. They were retreating for the first time since they steam-rollered out of Mother Russia into Central Europe during

World War II. Whether they are moving on orders from Moscow is not known.

A Hungarian peasant spat on one tank as it passed him an arm's length away. The Russian crew did not notice.

Hatred literally oozed from the Hungarians who silently lined the roadsides watching the Soviets evacuate Budapest.

The Russians were nervous but alert. They manned their one hundred millimetre tank cannon which were zeroed at the horizontal for firing straight ahead if necessary. And they held tightly to the handles of machine guns mounted in the tank cockpits and on truck tops.

Soon I came across the first signs of fighting.

Huge cannon holes punctured workers' houses. Windows were shattered.

A strange music filled the air – the tinkling of broken glass being trod on, driven on, swept aside.

Telephone and high tension wires hung crazily and tangled like wet spaghetti as if a hurricane had passed through. We reached a railroad crossing. The crossing gates appeared ridiculous, they were so unnecessary. No trains would be running on that railroad for some time.

Sleeping cars had been turned over as roadblocks. Their sides were stitched with machine-gun bullets, as if a giant sewing machine had methodically worked them up and down, zigzagged and come back for a final floral touch.

Now we ran into convoys of Hungarian trucks pressed into duty as ambulances and flying Red Cross flags. The doctors looked like butchers, so blood-spattered were their once-white aprons.

Trucks passed full of moaning wounded.

Then a truck with a large sign proclaiming 'Dead Bodies'.

The stench now was overpowering and as we neared the City the acrid smell of cordite also assailed our nostrils.

We were now in the Budapest suburbs, and more and more Soviet troops and tanks could be counted hurrying the wrong way.

I counted at least sixty Red Army tanks in one convoy.

They looked like circus elephants lumbering one behind the other, twitching from side to side as their heavy steel tracks slipped on debris or an oil slick.

'Budapest City Limits', the sign said, and with it came the distant chattering of machine guns.

An impressive-looking Soviet tankman blocked the road and waved us into a detour. 'Mopping up' operations were still going on.

A tank gun coughed in the distance and a split second later came a muffled concussion that pressured the eardrums. The crack of rifles sounded from snipers who would prefer to die rather than give up.

The street now was so littered I had to abandon the car. I began walking through the suburbs into a city of death.

There was Rakoczi Street, one of the main thoroughfares, leading down the bank of the gently flowing Danube. A Soviet tank was roaring down the street and I jumped quickly into a doorway with visions of vile-tempered Russians who fired cannon at men, boys, women and children only a few blocks from here. It passed and the tingling in my stomach subsided.

Hungarian women completely ignored the tank except for looks of such cold hatred that the emotion must have penetrated the steel side like X-rays. Trams, cars and battered trucks lay overturned in the streets as if by an irritable child who had scattered his toys with a blow of the hand.

Hungarian flags flew proudly from the vacant windows of shell-scarred houses. And all were minus the hated Communist Red Star which first appeared on the postwar Hungarian tricolor when the Soviets took over.

The Red Star was scissored out, slashed out, burned out.

Chalked signs were everywhere – 'Russians go'. One brownish-reddish slogan on a wall appeared to have been written in blood.

I passed a crowd happily hacking souvenir scraps from a giant bronze boot – part of the mammoth Josef Stalin monument toppled from its base last Tuesday night, cut with welders' torches and beaten to pieces – even to the walrus moustache.

A sort of cease fire appeared to be in operation this morning, as Soviet troops slowly withdrew.

Few here believe the 'Titoite' Government of Premier Imre Nagy, who was installed in the first dawn of the Revolution, can survive.

Some solution will have to be worked out before the day is out, or the bloodletting will certainly begin again.

Hungarians were pitifully friendly with me. As soon as anyone heard English a crowd gathered.

Men and women shook my hand and pounded me on the back. 'Good, Good,' they shouted.

I walked into an already jammed hotel and, with little hope of success, asked for a room.

'If you are Western, we'll find you a room even if we are full,' the clerk promised.

I got the room.

The Duna Hotel is on the banks of the Danube which divides Buda from Pest. Having secured my base, my immediate problem was to find a way of communicating with London, or for that matter with anywhere in the West, so that I could transmit my story. I was fortunate to hit paydirt, as my American colleagues reported it, by discovering a lone telex machine still working in the deserted Ministry of Foreign Affairs.

I pressed a key and it reacted.

So I dialled the UPI in London, and got through. I immediately locked the door and laboriously pumped out my story. It took me well over an hour, and it proved to be the first communication out of the beleaguered capital for more than two days. It scooped the world.

Later, I would receive the log on the day's activities at UPI. It read, 'No story in recent months has received such smash play as Cavendish's exclusive out of Budapest on 10/29.' For a journalist it was a great moment.

My next story, sent on the same wire, which nobody else had

93

yet discovered, was logged as follows: 'Tony Cavendish's despatch on Soviet troops leaving Budapest carrying their dead with them was one of the outstanding in weeks. Real sight, smell, sound stuff. It was plastered across the top of page one in papers across the country.'

But then my telex line was cut and the only way to get a story out was to drive to Vienna. This I did on 30 October, a Tuesday. I spent the night in the Bristol and had an enormous sirloin steak. (There was an element of guilt involved in that meal, Budapest was already very low on food.) Then, armed with large amounts of cash, I settled into a rented Opel and drove back to Budapest, in time for the real battle to start.

I had teamed up with Basil Davidson, for the *Daily Herald* and UPI were not competitors. During the fighting at the end of the first phase of the revolt we had worked our way down Ferenc Street and into the Kilian Barracks. Surrounding the barracks was a mighty ring of Russian tanks, field guns and mortars.

The attack on the barracks was heavy but was not an all-out assault. Machine guns barked, cannon thundered and the dull, deadly thump of mortars filled the air.

Blackened and smashed Soviet field guns, burned-out trucks and a burned Soviet tank littered the grounds. Small-arms fire whistled and a Red Army self-propelled gun roared down the street.

As it zoomed past, it let fly with its cannon. The blast blew flying splinters of stone and grit into my doorway.

One freedom fighter insisted that the men inside the barracks would never surrender.

'They will die there, or the Russians will go.'

The man told me also that the fighters inside believed the Russians would shoot them anyway if they came out, and that therefore they had nothing to lose.

On every side, people asked me what was happening in the United Nations. 'What are Britain and America doing?' they asked. 'Send us some *Panzer-faust* [bazookas] and we will soon get rid of the Russians.'

When Basil and I came back to our car we found this notice pinned to the windshield, 'For the reporter of the United Press. We can give you this information, the members of the AVH [Secret Police] were all paid 10,000 florins [$900] as well as their normal pay before the battles started. We found one of them and lynched him in the Ring Street and stuffed the money we found on him in his mouth.'

This message was signed, 'From the two young architects you talked to at the graves of the fallen young in the Karolotzi Garden.'

Radio Budapest reported that all fighting was finished but this was not true. Fighting was still going on and people insisted that it would go on until the Russians left.

In the Karolotzi Garden I had stopped at the graves of three fifteen year-old youngsters – two boys and a girl – shot down by Russian troops in the battle for Budapest. In Bakats Square I saw the body of an old man lying in the carved doorway of a church, carried there by friends who had no time to bury him.

Davidson and I later returned to the barracks during a lull in the fighting. There we met the commander, already a legend of the revolution, Colonel Pal Maleter.

After the Soviet withdrawal, we returned to talk with Colonel Maleter who asked me to go as his emissary to see Cardinal Mindszenty, and beg him to give a lead to the revolt.

The Roman Catholic Primate of Hungary received me in the small study of his Palace. He was a sick-looking man, with rheumy, tearful eyes. He talked to me about his desire for a Christian Democratic Hungary but refused to give a sign to the people as Maleter wanted. I reported this back to Maleter who advised me that he and General Istvan Kovacs had negotiated the complete withdrawal of Soviet troops from Hungary. He said a final meeting to confirm this was scheduled for 10 p.m. on Saturday, 3 November. It began to look as if the Hungarians might have pulled it off.

By this time we were quite a crew in the Duna. Journalists present included Tom (Sefton) Delmer of the *Daily Express*, Noel Barber of the *Daily Mail* and, of course, Basil Davidson.

Meals in the Duna dining room were becoming a ritual, and Tom Delmer held court round a large window table in the dining room, at which lavish amounts of plum brandy came and went.

Delmer had rendered important service during the war in the

field of black propaganda. He was the brains behind 'Soldatensender Calais', a German Forces radio network run by the British which put out all kinds of disinformation. The network was located in Aspley Guise and Milton Bryant, in properties requisitioned from the Duke of Bedford. Delmer got an OBE for his wartime work; though most people in the know thought that it rated at least a CMG or a knighthood. The politician Dick Crossman took most of the glory that was rightly Tom's.

Despite his occasional rudeness, I grew to like Tom and he eventually became a close friend of mine. We generally spoke to each other in German, since both of us thought we spoke it perfectly, and we generally called each other *'Herr Geheimrat'* (Mr Privy Councillor). In due course I introduced Delmer to Maurice Oldfield and he was able to do intelligence a few more favours before he died in 1979. Now it seems that apparently even Tom Delmer is open to suspicion. News comes that a young writer called Anthony Glees has joined the packed ranks of instant experts on intelligence matters and is claiming that Delmer worked for the Soviets.

After lunch on Friday, 2 November, Davidson and I spent two hours in the Parliament building with Deputy Premier Zoltan Tildy. Davidson had many Social Democratic contacts, particularly with Anna Kethly, a right-wing Social Democrat imprisoned from 1950 to 1954 who was to become a minister in the new Hungarian government.

Zoltan Tildy and Anna Kethly, both leaders of the new Hungary, assured us that the Russians were lying when they said Soviet troops were pulling out. Although I had seen columns of Soviet tanks heading away from Budapest, Zoltan assured us that this was just window dressing. As Dmitri Chepilov, former editor of *Pravda* and now Soviet Foreign Minister, announced to the world that no Soviet units had arrived in Hungary during the past sixty-four hours, the United States legation in Budapest cabled the lie to this to Washington. Columns of Soviet trucks with numbers prefixed by D4 and D6, not previously in Hungary, were already crossing the frontier carrying Tartar troops.

Tildy received us at the Parliament building wearing a well-pressed blue suit. Bodyguards with Thompson sub-machine guns stood watch by the doors. We talked about why the Soviet troops appeared to be withdrawing when there were reports of new troops arriving in Hungary in their thousands.

Tildy said 'several hundred' tanks had arrived from the Ukraine in the past forty-eight hours. These were now two hundred kilometres inside Hungary's frontier.

We asked about a new free Hungarian government made up of the Smallholders party, the Social Democrats and others.

'The Communist Party had collapsed,' Tildy said. Then Premier Imre Nagy called some of us to help him. Maleter, now a General, was with him. Nagy asked us what we thought United States reaction would be to a return of the Soviet forces, and we asked Maleter if his men would fight.

'That will depend on the officers,' he answered.

Meanwhile, Radio Free Europe continued to broadcast encouragement to the revolutionaries.

At the American legation things were happening. The uprising had caught the legation without its head man. Spencer Barnes was Chargé d'Affaires, but now Tom Wailes, a minister, had arrived, just back as Ambassador from Pretoria.

At 10 p.m. Wailes sent his first report to Foster Dulles in Washington: The city is ringed by Soviet troops, and many reports, not fully confirmed, say fresh Soviet troops advancing on Budapest.

At 4.30 a.m. on the morning of Sunday, 4 November, I was wakened by a transatlantic telephone call. It was Toronto Radio station wanting an eye-witness account from me on the situation in Budapest. Even as we were speaking a terrific artillery barrage started and the darkness in my room was lit by gunfire from the west. I dressed quickly and stared out of the window. About an hour after this Soviet T-54 tanks began to pull up in the street outside the hotel.

It was time to see if the Red Army was really returning. It was. I went out into the streets with Davidson. We decided to move over to the British legation and shelter there until we could discover which way the wind was blowing. Once there, I prepared another despatch which would be ready to send if I could find a means. It set out the situation as I saw it.

97

The smell of death hangs over Budapest. Hunger and disease stalk the living.

More than 200,000 Soviet troops – equal to 15 full Red Army Divisions – now hold shattered Hungary in their grip. Yet last ditch rebels fight on against the Red invader, and the bodies of freedom fighters and dead Russians lie in the streets.

Around me the crump of Russian artillery fire shook the ruins. Smoke rose from still burning buildings. Every now and then the crack of a rebel guerrilla's rifle shot rang out, followed by the boom of Russian tank guns and the staccato rattle of Soviet machine-gunners.

In alleyways, in darkened streets and from the glassless windows of shattered buildings, the fight went on.

The steel-sided tank against the sniper bullet. It was desperate youngsters who sprung up as fast as others were cut down: it was flaming bottles of gasoline against armour and big guns.

It was suicide to be a Red Army infantryman in that kind of battle without quarter.

Soviet Headquarters in Budapest was established in the Hungarian Defence Ministry. The Soviet Commandant was a Major General Grebennik. No one seemed to know his first name – as if it mattered.

But the mastermind behind the Red Army's efforts to crush Hungary was generally believed to be Marshal Georgi Zhukov himself, conqueror of Berlin, hero of the Soviet Union, Soviet Defence Minister.

Westerners estimated that crack armoured units made up 80 per cent of the Red Army troops throughout Hungary.

The Soviets launched their attack early morning at 4.50 a.m. On that same Sunday, 4 November, a thunderous artillery barrage crashed into the old city around the former Royal Castle on the west side of the Danube.

A heavy Red Army battery perched on Gellert Hill, overlooking the city, blasted Hungarian rebel strong points.

Elephantine T-54 tanks with 100 millimetre cannon lumbered into the streets of the city, only half-awake and unaware of the torture it still faced. Within an hour the Russians occupied all main centres and the bridges across the broad Danube river.

Major General Pal Maleter, hero of the first rebel stand at Kilian Barracks and now Hungarian Defence Minister, was away at Soviet Headquarters negotiating a settlement with the Russians.

A Soviet officer marched up to the main door of the Kilian Barracks and demanded entry. A rebel sentry opened the door, and was shot dead on the spot.

Red Army tanks converged on the yellow stone building, already pock-marked from the earlier fighting. The tanks opened point-blank fire. Within an hour the barracks was blazing and more than three hundred of the seven hundred original defenders were either dead or dying.

Directly in the line of fire was a children's clinic, with more than two hundred sick youngsters in it. Doctors and nurses sent out increasingly desperate pleas to spare the building. But the Red Army gunners were deaf to the appeals.

Hospital authorities telephoned the British legation, which in turn appealed to the Soviet Embassy. The Red Embassy replied that it could 'do nothing'. Red Army guns continued to fire right through the clinic, as nurses and doctors sought to shield screaming children. In an hour the building was a shambles, piled deep with the mangled bodies of children and staff. How many were killed there never was known, but it is certain that few escaped.

And still, in the midst of a battle raging all around them, old women, wrapped in black shawls, scurried through the ruins and smoke seeking a cabbage or a loaf of bread to feed their starving families. The young were all out fighting. Or their bodies lay mangled in the streets were Soviet tanks drove over them. Almost all had been shot down by the tank guns.

Outside the dingy old Duna Hotel on the Danube, headquarters of all foreign correspondents in Budapest, the crumpled body of a man in a green hunting cape lay sprawled on the pavement.

On the house opposite flew the green-white-red tricolor of Hungary with a large round hole where the communist Red Star had been cut out. A correspondent was about to tear down the flag to drape over the sprawled body when someone restrained him. The body was that of an AVO secret policeman chopped down in error by a Russian tank gun.

Western reporters put the Hungarian casualties in the first four days of the battle at around five thousand Hungarians and five hundred Russians. That may or may not have been true: most likely it is vastly exaggerated. But the world will probably never know the true toll of death in Budapest – let alone in the rest of Hungary – in a week that staggered the world.

The Russians blasted away a whole house to kill a single sniper. They pulverized the Korvin National Theatre. They put the historic former Royal Palace through a cannon meatgrinder. Even the Duna and Astoria Hotels came under shell-fire.

To add to the terror of the Hungarian population, many of the troops they used were Mongolian fighters from the steppes of innermost Asia, turned loose on a European city for the second time in eleven years.

Hungarian rebels desperately tore up paving blocks and ripped down street-car wires to pile into barricades, but the tanks flattened the barricades and the men behind them, then roared down on street lamps and signs and kept on their way.

Burnt-out cars remained where they had been shot up by the Red Army tanks.

Newsmen staying in the Duna Hotel were awakened that morning by the explosion of Soviet artillery and found all communications with the outside world severed. Almost a hundred in all, we hurried mainly for the shelter of the already crowded American, British, French legations and we bedded down mostly on cellar floors.

Josef Cardinal Mindszenty, the Roman Catholic Primate I had met on behalf of Pal Maleter, was given asylum at the US legation that morning, on special orders from Washington.

At the American legation, the first food was two peanut butter sandwiches; at the British legation, Consul Joan Fish organized the first proper meal – a typically British one of sausages and mashed potato for seventy-four people. Attaché Frances Forge issued bedding which consisted, in the main, of one blanket and space on the floor.

From our legations we could hear the close boom of cannon fire and the roar of MIG fighters spinning overhead as they poised to dive on the Kilian Barracks.

On the Tuesday following Sunday's attack, I picked my way through broken streets to the big Astoria Hotel on the inner ring. A department store next to it was burning and there were signs of looting – something Budapest had not experienced in the earlier battle during October.

Three Soviet tanks stationed in front of the Astoria were firing nearly point-blank into houses. They were answered by the occasional sniper fire.

A young girl with black hair and pale blue eyes, wearing a man's grey flannel pants many sizes too large, stopped me on the street and asked me to come to her shelter to see how the insurgents lived.

I followed her down to the dank cellar of an apartment house behind a shattered municipal building and found forty people, mostly women and children, crouched in the gloom and eating stale macaroni.

'We cannot make a fire,' one woman said. 'We've been here two days already. We have no more food, our men are fighting – what is left for us?' I had no answer. All I could do was forlornly give them the cigarettes I had with me and an unopened bar of chocolate. They took both.

That same day both the Yugoslav and Egyptian legations came under shell-fire and a Yugoslav diplomat was killed.

In the afternoon I moved out from the welcome but hard floors of the British legation and set up shop again in the Duna Hotel. The room opposite mine had previously been occupied by Delmer, who left for Vienna just before the fighting began. It had received a direct hit and was a shambles.

I typed my new stories among unwashed plates, pieces of old salami, crusts of stale bread and dripping, slowly drying-out nylon shirts. I could not file my despatches because there was still no communication with the outside world. There was also no heat, and the windows of my room were broken.

On Wednesday – the next day – the Soviet Commandant issued a proclamation demanding immediate surrender, but the fight raged on unabated.

A Red Army major announced that the Kremlin bosses had ordered shelling to continue until white flags hung from all the windows in Budapest. But the only flags to be seen were the hacked-about green-white-red Hungarian tricolors or black flags of mourning.

On the morning of Thursday, 8 November, I left Budapest by car with my despatches in an attempt to bring the first story of the battle to the West.

The car was mine, but I thought I would have a better chance if I took some company. I asked Basil Davidson, with whom I had started this adventure, to come with me and we agreed that Ernest Leiser, an American CBS correspondent, should join us. We called at the Soviet Embassy to ask Ambassador Yuri Andropov to issue us with a safe conduct pass. We were assured that there was no need for anything like that, we were free to go.

As we left Budapest, heading north towards the Czech frontier, a Red Army sentry loosed off several rounds of machine-gun fire at us, but missed. Having seen poor Noel Barber wounded by a trigger-happy Russian in Budapest, we were pleased to be on our way. We eventually reached Leled safely but, although we had valid Czech visas, the border guards refused to let us enter the country, and accused us of being counter-revolutionaries.

We had to do something, so we spent the night at Szob with some Hungarian railway workers, all pro-communist, but fiercely anti-Soviet. They made us welcome, and shared their food with us. 'The West should have helped us more,' one of them told us.

'Radio Free Europe encouraged us, then the West let us down.' It was hard not to agree.

We left early next morning and took the ferry over the Danube at Esztergom. We drove on until we came to a roadblock at Györ, where we were immediately arrested. The guards ordered us out of the car, which was promptly confiscated. Everything else was taken, our papers, my despatches, our cameras, film, everything. We were put under house arrest in a hotel and told that we would be held until orders about us were received.

A little while later we were separated and for two hours I was interrogated by a couple of KGB majors. What have I seen, who have I talked to, who sent me to Budapest in the first place and why did I say I was only a journalist? The questioning was firm – sometimes hard – and repetitive, but I got the impression the situation was still not clear to the Russians themselves.

I argued with them, refusing to pay my living expenses which they were demanding while I was held. 'Fine,' they said, 'the Hungarian community can pay them,' and they summoned the mayor to inform him that the community was now financially responsible for the arrested journalists.

On the third day, one of the KGB majors suddenly appeared and announced that we could go. We needed no second bidding but retrieved the car and our possessions and raced for the frontier and on to Vienna.

There is a sting in the tail to this story.

Years later I was told by Maurice that the Service had intercepted and deciphered a Soviet radio signal about the group of journalists being held in Györ. A KGB major general had been ordered to fly from Moscow to interrogate one of them on whom they had records. But we were allowed to leave, by mistake, before the general arrived. Maurice thought it probable they had identified me as a former MI6 officer.

The following extract is taken from an American editorial in the leading newspaper of Salt Lake City.

It is hoped that readers of the remarkable eyewitness story
and diary of Anthony Cavendish printed on the opposite

page will pause a moment to realize that men get killed getting stories like that.

Three of them have been killed the past week seeking just such stories, two of them in Egypt, one in Budapest.

This is the price dedicated men are willing to risk to bring truth to the world.

It is because of such dedication that men who would dictate to their countrymen must first pull down a curtain behind which no free newspaperman can go. Deception and savagery, those twins of dictatorship, cannot survive in the light. Wherever reporters find it possible to learn and write about such atrocities as the gutting of the children's hospital that Mr Cavendish describes, dictatorship cannot last. And wherever such opportunities do exist, reporters *will* report them, regardless of the personal danger involved. That is the creed of the profession.

There are in these observations, it seems to us, two immediate lessons for the American people.

One is that most Americans ought to be thoroughly ashamed of the apathy with which they regard the closing of doors in their own government. The newspapermen who risk bullets and mobs for stories from strife-torn parts of the world do so for the same ideals as those who seek to know what is going on in a school board or a congressional committee meeting. Both are working for your right to know. Both deserve your support.

The other lesson is that the death of these three men, and many others like them in years gone by, makes a mockery of the State Department's publicly announced reasons for not letting newsmen enter Red China. The objection has been that it would be too risky. But most reporters are dedicated to the ideal that truth is worth great risk. They are ready when the door is opened.

CHAPTER 13

I LEFT HUNGARY remembering the many instances of bravery I had witnessed in the previous ten days and how people who had gone into Hungary as dedicated communists had realized that their belief in the Soviets was based on a false premise. The utter ruthlessness and savagery which the Red Army used to put down a revolt within the Soviet system said more to the world about Soviet methods in ten days than other events had in the previous ten years.

I took with me the memory of my meeting in the Soviet Embassy with Yuri Andropov on the day that I left Budapest, and his bland assurance that no safe conduct was needed. He was later to become Head of the KGB and, after that, Chairman of the Central Committee and, in his day, the most powerful man in Russia.

I tried to analyse whether there was anything more I could have done and whether I had behaved in the right way when faced with quite considerable dangers.

I remember walking from the Duna Hotel up to a bridge close by where a Russian tank suddenly began machine-gunning buildings on the southern side of the bridge. I was with Basil Davidson who calmly turned around and together we walked back to the hotel. All the time I wondered whether we were going to get a bullet in our own backs, and I would certainly not have put on such a languid air if I had not been with Davidson.

Similarly, the threat of serious KGB interrogation had worried me during the time we were held in Győr. I had been briefed on interrogation by the Service and was quite happy standing up to the KGB officers when their attacks on me were only verbal, but I shuddered to think of what could have happened had they begun to use drugs or electric shock on me.

I was soon to discover that friends of mine had contacted my KGB journalist friend, Saplin, in Paris, and asked him to intervene on my behalf while I was imprisoned in Győr. I was anxious to determine whether Saplin had done anything – either positively or negatively.

I had done him various favours and had even taken him to SHAPE Headquarters at Versailles for lunch, making him the first Soviet correspondent to go there. He had asked me to arrange it, and, having checked with Brigadier Lionel Cross whether it was in order for me, as an accredited correspondent, to bring a fellow journalist to the Headquarters for lunch, had received the go-ahead. We met the first of the German officers to arrive at SHAPE at that time, Colonel Graf Adolf von Kielmanseg, later Commander of the Allied Forces in Central Europe.

Additionally, Saplin and I had spent several wild drinking evenings together, along with a Roman Catholic priest, a friend of mine who was in touch with the Algerian revolutionaries, and various other friends who inhabited that twilight world peopled by journalists, criminals and members of the intelligence services.

I was surprised when I later made a telephone call to Paris, to be told that Saplin had died suddenly, but all this I only established a couple of days later.

It was thus with enormous relief that I arrived in Vienna from Győr and booked into the Hotel Bristol on the Ring, where I soaked for a long time in a hot bath. I then ordered an *entrecôte* steak as large as could be produced by the hotel, and settled down to a long sleep. I could not have been in bed for more than two hours when the Vienna office telephoned to say that New York was asking for further stories from me.

The history of the United Press is entitled *Deadline Every Minute*, and that is just how it was. Somewhere in the world one of its clients (and there were around five thousand of them) was going to print and needed the latest news to update its story. These stories always had to be written in such a way that if 'a Kansas City milkman' read them, he would get the up-to-date picture of the whole situation covered by the story.

From Vienna I flew back to London to congratulations, various lunches from members of the UP hierarchy, and, importantly, a welcome salary increase. I was also nominated for various journalistic prizes and it was decided that I should now be based permanently in Eastern Europe. So a week later I flew back to Warsaw where my standing, certainly with Polish journalists, and others I had met who were interested in events in Budapest, had changed for the better; although the opposite was true for my relationship with the bureaucrats I had to deal with in the Ministry of Foreign Affairs.

Monday, 19 November 1956 dawned cold and bleak in Warsaw. The sky was overcast, one could barely see the top of the hideous Modern Palace of Science and Culture, the temperature was one degree above freezing, and people who had no cause to be out huddled indoors around radiators and hot water pipes for warmth.

But it was not a normal day.

'They come back today,' the liftman said to me, as I went down to the dining room.

'Do you think we will be all right?' asked the young girl in the reception office.

People gathered everywhere in the coffee rooms to discuss *'them'*. For Wladyslaw Gomulka, Aleksander Zawadzki, Cyrankiewicz and Stefan Jedrychowski were to return that afternoon from Moscow from a visit which would decide the future of Poland.

A month earlier Khrushchev had arrived in Warsaw out of the blue to lay down the law to the VIIIth plenum of the Polish Peoples United Workers (Communist) Party and to Gomulka.

That day, 10 October, climaxed the Polish struggle for independence from Moscow, which began with the strike of the Zispo factory workers in Poznan on 26 June.

For the past four months the cauldron had simmered, the Stalinists (the Natolin group, after the area of Warsaw in which they had their sumptuous villas) had been pushed more and more on to the defensive, and then the VIIIth plenum brought Gomulka back into power as First Secretary of the Party, and Khrushchev's opposite number in Poland. Gomulka had won the first round. But this visit to Moscow, what would it bring?

Many workers had begged their hero not to go, for, after Hungary, they feared he would not return. But Gomulka went all the same. The delegation returned from Moscow by special train and, as soon as they crossed the frontier into Poland at Brest, peasants stormed the train to hear what had been achieved.

The four leaders of the delegation promptly sent off a telegram to their hosts, Messrs Khrushchev, Voroshilov and Bulganin, in which they used all the old phrases, 'esteemed and dear comrades', 'warm greetings and expressions of gratitude', 'cordial and friendly reception' and finally 'long live friendship and brotherhood between the Polish people and the peoples of the Soviet Union'. But they had their tongues in their cheeks after winning the second round of the struggle for independence.

For that is what they did. They got nothing new out of the Soviet leaders, but they did get acceptance of the status quo — complete Polish sovereignty, and control of Soviet troop movements in Poland.

At twenty minutes to six in the evening, their special train steamed into platform three at Warsaw Central Station, where a crowd of several thousand, including foreign ambassadors, journalists and officials, awaited them.

Warsaw station was then an open air affair and not what one would expect to be the main station of a capital city. Short shelters ran along the first fifty yards of the platforms, leaving the traveller open to the biting winds, and partly to rain and snow.

Yet an hour before Gomulka's arrival the crowds were there, shivering and jabbering to each other about what the future would bring. The officials, and journalists in the know, sought shelter in the small *salon d'honneur* decorated with red and white carnations, and containing some excellent imitation Louis XIV furniture.

I chatted there with Witold Nowierski, the Prime Minister's press secretary, but he revealed little, since Polish officials were always loath to give the foreign press information.

As the time drew near for the train's arrival, the ambassadors arrived. Joe Jacobs and Sir Eric Berthoud arrived together both muffled up to the ears, and looking as expectant as the Poles. Foreign Minister Adam Rapacki too was looking happy as he turned up and took his place at the head of the platform.

And in steamed the train.

Flash bulbs popped, klieg lights glared and suddenly every-body was waving and shouting, and then they started to sing '*Sto La Sto La*', the Polish 'For he's a jolly good fellow', which actually means, 'May he live a hundred years'.

First out was Gomulka, in overcoat and trilby hat, followed by Cyrankiewicz and the rest of the delegation. They were immediately enveloped in the crowd and walked down the platform to the small station yard to the cheering crowd.

A small platform had been erected and they climbed on to it for Gomulka to say:

Dear Comrades and Citizens! On behalf of the delegation I thank you for the welcome we are now witnessing. The numerous, spontaneously assembled crowds of people on all the railway stations, from Terespol to here in Warsaw, are the best approval of the correctness of the Government policy and express the acceptance of the results of our talks in Moscow.

These results are contained in the published declaration and are known to all in Poland. During our four days' stay in Moscow, during meetings and talks with Soviet Comrades, all the problems which had accumulated for years have been settled.

The leaders of the Soviet State and of the Communist Party of the Soviet Union, who received us very cordially as representatives of the nation, have wiped out everything that was anomalous and incorrect in past Polish–Soviet relations. They decided, among other things, to cover all our claims arising out of our mutual trade in the past by cancelling the large debt amounting to over 2,000,000,000 roubles, contracted by Poland.

At this point in events a drunken railway worker, who had clambered up on to the wall of the yard, shouted, 'Three cheers for Gomulka,' and the whole crowd let loose with an ear-splitting roar.

They had already read in the papers that the Russians had given so much wheat and so much cash, but they wanted to hear it from Gomulka's own lips and see him in person before they believed it.

'What a man is our Wieslaw,' said an old woman next to me, who was quite happily being pushed and shoved by the excited crowd.

At last Gomulka was able to go on:

All the obstacles on the road towards increasing Polish–Soviet friendship, a friendship not resulting from a Government order but coming from the hearts and minds of the Polish nation, have been removed.

We have talked with representatives of the Communist Party of the Soviet Union and of the Soviet Government as two parties with equal rights, imbued with a spirit of socialism common to us and with a spirit of good-neighbourly, fraternal relations between the Polish nation and the nation of the Soviet Union.

Comrades! Let us develop these friendly relations so necessary to us as well as to our great Eastern neighbour the Soviet Union.

So much for the speech. The party newspaper described what happened when Gomulka finished as a 'long-lasting ovation', which was an understatement. Most of the newsmen who were there agreed that they had not seen such a welcome before. Certainly, I had not.

As Gomulka ended, our drunken cheer leader jumped down from his place on the wall and bulldozed his way through the crowd to try and shake Gomulka's hand. But so solid was the crowd that he did not make it. But he went on calling for cheers, and wishing Gomulka and the other delegates long life.

Cyrankiewicz, always the perfect politician, patted a small girl on the head when she presented him with a bouquet. 'The flowers we take,' he said. 'The child we give back.' The people roared with laughter. Then the leaders of new Poland, forcing their way through the dense throng, moved over to the black limousines for the ride to their homes.

But the railway worker was not to be thwarted in showing his own personal approval of what had been achieved in Moscow.

'Up with the cars,' he shrieked, as they moved slowly through the sardined people. And with one accord the people surged round Gomulka's car and lifted it completely off the ground. If they could, they would have carried him home that way, but ZIMs are heavy cars, and eventually the tired delegates were allowed to drive off, and the happy crowd dispersed slowly.

They had seen 'Wieslaw', they had heard him. He was back, and he had brought something for all of them. What was it he had brought back? The most tangible thing was the very generous Soviet offer of more than one million tons of wheat. Had Poland not been able to obtain this, she would have had to spend precious hard currency on getting it from Canada or elsewhere in the West. And there was also the Soviet promise of economic help in the future. Promises of credits in two years' time.

But the greatest thing that Gomulka achieved – and this was known to the people who crowded round him at the station – was that Moscow had accepted the fact that Gomulka was the leader of Poland, that the small dome-headed man they had thrown in jail was home to tell them that the Poles were masters in their own home. There had been considerable fear when the Government and Party group left for Moscow.

Strange things had happened before to visitors to the Kremlin: only some eight months earlier the Party First Secretary Boleslaw Bierut had died suddenly of a heart attack while attending the XXth Party Congress. In spite of the warnings, Gomulka went, and people in Poland knew that the Russians were risking a bigger and bloodier Poznan or Budapest if they touched him. And they knew it in Moscow too.

Poland was hemmed in on every side by the Red Army except to the north where the Baltic Sea rages. But an historic event buffered Gomulka, and wrecked the Kremlin's plans for bringing Poland back to heel. In Hungary the people of Budapest had determined to throw off the Soviet yoke which lay heavily on their shoulders. The Soviets did not want a second Budapest in Warsaw. They had seen the tremendous losses suffered by communist parties all over the world because of the Soviet intervention in Hungary; and later there had been vicious battles within the parties within the communist empire. The Poles had made it clear that, having gone as far as they had, they would not give up everything without a fight.

Although the Polish delegation had signed a joint declaration in Moscow which regulated 'mutual relations on the Leninist principles of equality', the Soviet leaders were intent on returning to the previous status of keeping Poland a dependent nation, when next the Poles required economic help.

Hungary stopped that. And it can almost be said that Hungary's defeat was Poland's victory. The blood of the Hungarian people flowed for the benefit of Poland's freedom.

Gomulka at this time was at the zenith of his popularity, which was to decline slowly until the elections in January 1957.

That night, after meeting the delegation at the station, I sipped vodka with a Polish newspaperman who had travelled a lot in the West.

'Was that really a spontaneous reception for Gomulka,' I asked. 'Or were the people told to be there?'

'Of course, certain factory delegations were told to be there,' he said, and shrugged. 'But surely you could see that this time they really enjoyed welcoming him. And many people on their way home saw that crowd forming and joined in to give personal thanks to this man who stood up against the Russians. You must have seen that they were genuine in their feelings.'

I had to agree with him. They were.

One of the first tasks I had on behalf of UP was to settle an outstanding claim they had against the Polish Press Agency, which had originally been a client of UP – and still continued to take their service, and use it – even though it was many years since they had paid a subscription. The amount owing now ran into many tens of thousands of dollars and I saw that it would be unlikely, in the economic circumstances of the time, that they would pay in dollars. However, it did seem possible that they might agree to pay in zloty. In due course I obtained the total amount, although, as expected, it was paid in Polish currency and the amount had to be spent on UP expenses in Poland. Nevertheless, to have achieved a settlement where everyone else had failed was very satisfactory, although I realize that it had not been due to my eloquence but rather to the changing political situation.

In any event the money was now in the bank and would do nobody any good unless it was beneficially spent. It meant that UP could keep its man in Poland at virtually no cost until the funds ran out, and they certainly lasted for the remainder of my stay.

It soon became clear that under the new regime now run by Wladyslaw Gomulka and Cyrankiewicz, the tight-rope they had to walk put them in a precarious position, balancing so as not to upset Moscow excessively by wanting to improve relations with the West. Their means of doing this were primarily through the Western correspondents in Warsaw and using their press attachés and foreign correspondents abroad to seek to influence the domestic media.

There were not a large number of Western correspondents in Warsaw. There was, of course, the AP, the *New York Times,* the London *Times*, AFP,[1] Reuters, and regularly we were visited by foreign correspondents who flew in for visits of a few days, which they felt turned them into experts on the Polish scene.

During this time I became friendly with the British Air Attaché, a distinguished group captain with a DSO from his exploits in a Wellington bomber during the war, and his American colleague, a USAF lieutenant colonel who reminded me of Glen Miller because at heart he was really a trumpet player.

The amount of time I spent with these Western service personnel confirmed, in the eyes of the Polish UB (Intelligence Service) at least, that I was more than just a journalist; but since they considered all foreign journalists to be engaged in some sort of spying activity, this did not make much difference, particularly as in late 1956 and 1957 the Western press was being courted by the Government.

The most convenient way of living in Warsaw was in a hotel. So I settled into the Hotel Bristol in Room 105, which was enormous with a large bed in an alcove, and a bathroom with a bath in which one could have washed a medium-sized racehorse. I do not know when the hotel was built, but I would guess in the early 1920s. There was a concierge on each floor, who held the key and who took note of whoever entered or left a room. There was

---

[1] Agence France Presse.

also a large dining room where there were always two dishes that never ran out, *indyck* or *schinka* (turkey or ham). There was always a supply of Polish vodka, which I soon came to like and with which Russian vodka, in my opinion, does not compare.

My enormous bank balance of zloty meant that neither UP nor I had to worry about funding my stay or its costs, particularly telephone calls. There were, at this time, three different rates for the zloty. There was the official rate of four zloty to the dollar. Then there was the tourist rate of about four times that, and finally there was the PKO (hard currency shop) or black market rate of about 120 zloty to the dollar – or thirty times the official rate. Thus foreigners visiting Poland, and equipped with US dollar notes, were able to make a 3000 per cent profit if they exchanged them for local cash, and the best buy was the Russian copy of the Leica camera, called a Zorki, which could be obtained for 1500 zloty, or less than 15 US dollars.

My happiest memory of meeting people in Warsaw was of a visit made there in early 1957 by Yehudi Menuhin and his charming wife, Diana.

In her excellent book *Fiddler's Moll* Diana recalls our meeting, describing me as '. . . so British as to belong to a past backed by an Empire that ruled the waves'. One night I took the Menuhins to dine in the best small restaurant I had found, close to the Polish Press Club, a place much used for a meeting place by Polish intellectuals and artists. As we prepared to tuck into our *indyck*, other patrons of the restaurant started to come over and bow low to the maestro, and pay their compliments, or to say how thrilled they were that Yehudi had come to Poland to give concerts there.

The Menuhins, like myself, stayed in the Hotel Bristol but were unfortunate in having the Royal suite with its decayed grandeur and inefficient and unhygienic lavatory, which Yehudi had to unblock with his travelling music stand.

On their departure from Warsaw by train, Diana describes in her book how they looked back and saw me on the platform standing 'like a lighthouse in a rocky sea'.

During my stay, my friendship with the various service attachés ensured that I was privy to the intelligence games of cops and robbers they played with the local State Security officers. Since the service attachés had diplomatic status and were permitted to travel widely – although there were certain restricted areas – they were generally on the move, watching manoeuvres or seeking to photograph new pieces of Soviet military equipment.

On one occasion the American Air Attaché asked if I would let him drive me home one evening for dinner, then leave his house about dawn, wearing his uniform cap, and drive off in his CD car; the tail normally behind him wherever he went would therefore be led astray, so that the attaché could then be picked up by his British colleague a little later. The British attaché had also arranged to ditch his tail, and they were able to get out of Warsaw undetected. The plan worked successfully, but it was yet another black mark awarded to me by the Polish security authorities.

I used to travel myself quite a lot and I always had a camera with a couple of lenses with me. If I was able to take a surreptitious photograph of anything of interest, I did so and passed it on.

The highlight of journalistic stays in Poland were the grand diplomatic receptions given for visiting Soviet leaders and Heads of State. I was one of two correspondents standing with Chinese Prime Minister Chou En Lai at a reception given in his honour, where he made his now famous 'Let all the flowers blossom' remark on being questioned by us about different communist theories propagated since the Hungarian Revolution.

I took advantage of my talks with Chou En Lai, who spoke good French, to ask him if I could visit China, as, at this time, no correspondent representing any of the American media had been allowed to visit China. Chou summoned his press secretary, Madame Kung Peng, who I believe was also Head of the Press Department of the Foreign Ministry, and who it was rumoured was also Chou's mistress. He instructed her that I was to be given a visa and be allowed to visit China, and that when I was in Peking, she should arrange for me to see him again.

I promptly wired the good news to UP, who said that I should apply immediately for a visa since they obviously felt Chou was far more newsworthy than Poland.

For the next three years, while I was still in the UP, I applied for that elusive visa about every three months in various different capitals, but it never came through and the nearest I ever got to Peking was to be called UP's correspondent designate for the People's Republic of China.

Two of the most impressive men I have ever met were Chou En Lai and Marshal Tito. Both of them exuded that sort of power that I imagine people feel in the presence of a messiah, but they were very different; Chou, an educated intellectual from the Mandarin class, and Tito, a lifelong worker and communist. But their exceptional qualities of leadership were, I suppose, similar to those that Churchill had. The only Englishman I ever met who approached their standard was Harold Macmillan.

In the spring of 1957 – although there had been elections in the country and although Gomulka, who had been imprisoned under the Stalinist regime, was now at the helm again – dissatisfaction broke out throughout Poland and surfaced in the industrial town of Lodz. The tramway operators went on strike and the police went into action against them. One of my informants, in whom I had great trust, passed me a message saying no more than I should go quickly and in secret to Lodz. I had to make a quick decision and decided I would take his advice, got into my car and drove to Lodz, where I arrived about 7 o'clock in the evening. Around me there were ugly scenes of rioting and the battle was causing considerable damage. I immediately phoned out a report, which caught the world headlines.

As a result of my coverage of this event I hit the headlines myself, because I was summoned to the Ministry of Foreign Affairs and told I was no longer *persona grata* with the Polish Government. I was given seven days to leave the country.

Since I was being expelled from the country, it was obviously necessary to collect what belongings I had in the Hotel Bristol, and pack them into the back of my car. So I advised the authorities that I would be leaving Warsaw, taking the road to the Czech border and then carrying on via Prague to wherever I was going. In fact I thought I might stay in Prague and might even make it my new base.

On the day of my departure I went down to the garage and saw a couple of secret police waiting next to my car, in a Pobeda car.

As I drove off they fastened to the tail of my car where they remained until I reached the Czech border.

Entering Czechoslovakia I produced my passport and a Czech visa permitting me a fourteen-day stay. I had obtained this in the Czech Consulate in Warsaw some time back. It was always useful to have at least one or two valid visas from Eastern bloc countries in your passport, and these could be updated as they expired. After a cursory search of my car and after my passport had been carefully examined and stamped, I was waved through and drove into Prague to the Alcron Hotel.

I filled in the registration form, handed over my passport and went up to my room, which was considerably more comfortable than my old one in Warsaw.

My stay in Prague lasted only until early the following morning when two gentlemen presented themselves at the door of my room and produced their identity cards, which proclaimed them to be members of the State Security Service. They handed me my passport, advised me that my visa had been cancelled and told me I was not welcome in the Czechoslovakian Socialist Republic. They also told me to leave Czechoslovakia that day.

I telephoned my masters in UP in London, and told them that the Czechs did not want me, so we settled on my going to Belgrade, where two friends from my journalistic days in Paris now occupied senior positions.

Leaving Czechoslovakia I drove into Germany, from Germany down through Austria and entered Yugoslavia over the Loibl Pass, and then took the motorway from Zagreb to Belgrade, where I settled into the Moscow Hotel.

I still had a valid visa for Bulgaria in my passport and I thought I might be able to get away with a quick trip there before they too closed their doors to me. A meeting of the International Olympic Committee was scheduled to be held in Bulgaria, and there would be other journalists attending who I thought might get the authorities to give me the benefit of the doubt, if the Bulgarian Security Service were thinking of showing themselves unhappy at my presence. The Bulgarian representative on the Olympic Committee was an admirable septuagenarian, a former Cavalry General, and the representative from Iran was Prince Reza, the

Shah's brother. The Hungarian delegate was a timid little gentleman, accompanied by his glamorous daughter. Much of the
discussion over drinks was about the sad days of Budapest the
previous year.

I filed several 'general interest' stories from Bulgaria and then
flew back to Belgrade in a rickety Soviet copy of a DC3. I spent the
next six months working in Belgrade. The UP then decided I
should return to London in order to await my visa to China – for
we had still not given up hope. In the meantime I could be
deployed from London to wherever there was a good story
breaking.

CHAPTER 14

MY NEXT INTERESTING ASSIGNMENT revolved around Beirut, where, in the summer of 1958, the Americans sent in their Marines. The King of Iraq was about to be assassinated and the troubles in Cyprus were at their height, with Archbishop Makarios at the centre, but I only got to Beirut by accident.

We had no correspondent in Amman, and so, when the vibrations throughout the Middle East quickened, I was told to get myself to Amman and cover the situation from there. As is always the way in a growing international crisis, the first effects are on the airlines, who change or cancel their schedules. I had intended to travel by Sabena but found when I got to Brussels that the connection was cancelled. There was, however, a flight to Beirut which I took, reckoning that I was only in a neighbouring country and I should be able to get on to Amman with ease. However, by the time I got to Beirut all hell had been let loose there, so I was told by UP to stay and help out, and there I spent my next six weeks.

The UP journalists took over the top floor of a seafront hotel and arranged comfortable coverage from there of the battles that were raging in Beirut. We had a couple of telephones laid on to the swimming pool with cords long enough to reach to the water's edge.

We then acquired some car inner tubes which, when inflated, could support plastic trays which in turn could support our bottles of local beer and toasted sandwiches. We were then able to telephone in our vivid and convincing descriptions of the fighting going on in Lebanon while sitting in a swimming pool with our feet dangling in the water, drinking our drinks and eating our sandwiches.

My next move was to Baghdad. Word came that both the King and his Prime Minister, Nuri Pasha, had been assassinated. There seemed no way to get to Baghdad because the frontiers were closed and no aircraft were being permitted to land, so I went to see Selim Bey Salaam, one of the bosses of Middle East Airlines and the nephew of a prominent politician. I told Selim that I needed to get to Baghdad and asked if he would charter me a plane that could take off the minute the authorities opened Baghdad airport. He agreed to, and the charter fee for the flight there and back worked out about $2400. Selim also told me that his brother Salaam Salaam was an MEA pilot who would fly our plane.

I knew UP would not take kindly to me expending that sort of money on a trip by myself to Baghdad, even if it was to be the first trip in after the Revolution, so I decided to invite my colleagues to join in and share the expense. I sold twenty seats to other journalists in the DC3 for $200 each, thus making a profit on the flight and also getting myself and two UP colleagues on the trip for free!

It was on this trip that I renewed by friendship with Tom Delmer, whom I had first met and eventually come to admire in Budapest. Three days later, when we took off, Delmer occupied two seats on our DC3 and was still unable to get a seat belt around his massive girth.

When we landed at Baghdad the temperature was 105°F in the shade and, somehow or other, I persuaded somebody with a jeep to drive me into Baghdad. We were not able to find out a lot more to add to the radio broadcasts from Baghdad, but at least it enabled UP to put a Baghdad dateline on their stories, and, at that time, it seemed the dateline was sometimes more important than the story.

UP kept a correspondent in Moscow, which enabled them to put out Moscow stories from the BBC monitor of Moscow radio at Caversham, with a Moscow dateline on them, thus saving thousands of dollars in telegram, telephone and telex charges.

One great advantage of having the American Marines in Beirut was that we became accredited to their press officer, who could conjure up all the facilities offered to correspondents when the Americans were in action somewhere and wanted good press coverage. When there was a shortage of American cigarettes, the press officer advised us that we were perfectly at liberty to use the duty free shop on one of the American supply ships and buy what we wanted. When I indicated to him that it might be difficult getting out there, he offered to lay on a helicopter to take me down to the beach serving the landing craft which went to and fro from the vessels.

I took the helicopter he offered to the beach and boarded the landing craft, impressed with the way things were turning out. But when we got to the supply vessel my mood changed immediately, for I discovered I had to board the ship by a rope ladder going up her side, and that she was as high as a five-storey building. As she rolled one way in the sea, the rope ladder swung out, and as she rolled the other way the rope ladder swung back, crashing into the side of the ship. I arrived on deck battered and utterly exhausted.

Liquid refreshment was offered in the form of Coca Cola, and after a quick tour of the ship and a visit to the PX, I made the perilous journey down the rope ladder with a kind sailor following me and bringing my purchases. Arriving at the beach, the front of the landing craft was let down and, keen to cut an athletic figure, I jumped off the front of the craft and splashed down in the water, twisting my ankle and dropping my purchases.

A few nights later Larry Collins, who was UP's resident correspondent in Beirut, and who had brought with him a decrepit old Hillman Minx, suggested we visit a nightclub in the hills behind Beirut to see a girlfriend of his. We had a pleasant and stimulating evening, the stimulus being provided mainly by *arak*, fermented date juice. On our return downhill to Beirut, both of us the worse for *arak*, we swung around a corner and Larry, who was driving, just missed hitting a large American sedan jacked up with one of its rear wheels missing. We assumed, as it turned out we were supposed to, that the owner had gone off with his wheel to get a puncture repaired and would be back at some time to replace the wheel and drive off.

It seemed we had barely gone to our rooms when the telephone rang and one of our Lebanese stringers was on the line saying that an attempt to assassinate the Prime Minister had been made and that a black car parked on the Prime Minister's route from his home to his office had been packed with explosives and had just been detonated. Many people had been killed. I knew exactly what he was talking about and exactly which car had been packed with explosives.

I rushed out of the hotel, dressed only in a short-sleeved shirt and trousers, and took a taxi to the scene of the assassination attempt. True enough, the explosion was where I had supposed it would be and the road was strewn with wreckage and bodies.

Morning arrived and as the sun came up it started to burn my arms and face on which I had no covering. As the day got warmer the smell of the bodies began to produce that sickly sweet smell of death I had not known since Budapest. With my press accreditation I asked the police why, since ambulances were available, the bodies could not be removed. 'Ah,' one told me, 'we cannot move the bodies until the coroner comes, and as he was not home last night we cannot find him.'

It was not until mid-afternoon that the coroner appeared, by which time I had sores on my arms from the burning sun, from which I still bear the scars, and the smell of the dead bodies was nauseating.

I counted six bodies, none of them anything to do with the Prime Minister or his escort, but from a large car filled with the wife and children of the driver. There were six of them in the car and they had all been killed. My competitor filed a story saying there were seven, against my report saying there were six.

I later got a call from New York asking how AP had seven dead and had taken all the play in the US newspapers, when I had said there were only six. I reiterated in a telex that I said six because there were six, because I had counted them and been with them. But by then it was too late: editors prefer to use the story with the highest number of deaths.

I was about to return to London after the two revolutions had run their course, when I was told by UP to get over to Cyprus and attach myself to Archbishop Makarios. I had made a friendship during this period with Sir Anthony Nutting, who had resigned as Foreign Minister of State at the time of the Suez crisis in 1956. He was now correspondent for the New York *Herald Tribune* and I found him both a congenial and friendly companion. Anthony and I decided to go to Cyprus together. We arrived in Nicosia and shared a car into town. I was about to unpack my bag when I learned that the Archbishop was now in Athens where the final decisions about the future of Cyprus were to be made. Grabbing my things, I rushed out of the hotel to the airport and took the next plane to Athens, where the Archbishop was in conference with Prime Minister Konstantine Karamanlis.

After this I returned to London, where my masters had still not given up hope that one day I would get my elusive visa for Peking.

For a long time the financial mandarins of UP had wondered how they could profit from the massive private communications network which could transmit words and pictures around the globe far faster than was possible at that time for ordinary people in commerce.

It was decided I should become Commercial Manager of UP, and my task was to make money from selling the facilities of UP to commerce and industry. For example, when Vivian Fuchs made his historic visit to the South Pole, I was able to sell BP's advertising people a picture direct from the South Pole, which was used as the main BP advertisement of the time.

I travelled in Europe a great deal, and soon UP was undertaking assignments for companies like Krupp and Mannesmann, Shell and other oil companies, industrial giants and their advertising and PR agencies. Thus we covered, on a commercial basis, industrial happenings which did not merit normal press coverage. For example, we could photograph the drilling of a special well in Kenya and send in the picture and a lengthy caption within a few hours, whereas it would have taken an advertising agency two days at the minimum to have got the same picture and information.

This was also the beginning of the jet age, in the sense that the revamped Comet and the Boeing 707 opened up the transatlantic services of BOAC and Pan Am.

United Press were invited to send a correspondent on BOAC's inaugural flight and I joined Sir Basil Smallpiece, at that time BOAC's Managing Director, on the inaugural Comet flight across the Atlantic. I had talks with my bosses in New York and then flew back to London on one of BOAC's strato cruisers, having decided that my days in UP were nearing an end.

The excitement and expense-account living of the Army, spying and journalism had developed my tastes to an extent my income could not afford. From about £1 a day when I left the Army, to £650 a year when I left MI6, and now $75 a week, I still did not think I was doing very well. I decided, therefore, that as soon as an opportunity presented itself for making money, I should jump at it.

I had heard through contacts that a Czech engineer who had escaped from his country to the West was developing a new and revolutionary way of making a steel pipe at lower than conventional cost. With the imminent enormous expansion of the oil and gas industries, the manufacturing of steel line pipe was soon to be the name of the game. When I thus had the opportunity of helping the Czech establish his operation in the United States – at a starting salary four times greater than that I was getting from UP, and with the glamorous-sounding title of Vice President – I took leave of UP. They had taught me a great deal, and I left with their blessing and an offer to take me back whenever and if ever I wanted.

CHAPTER 15

I ARRIVED IN the United States in October 1959 on a BOAC
Comet IV, and put up in New York at the St Moritz Hotel
overlooking Central Park. I re-established contact with my friends
at the UP, then set off for Milwaukee, where I was met by a private
De Havilland Dove, the property of an American with whom I was
going to work to exploit marketing possibilities for the steel pipe
invented by my Czech friend. My schedule soon settled down into
a routine ten days at our Headquarters in Manitowoc, Wisconsin,
ten days travelling over the whole of the United States and Canada
and then ten days in New York.

Not long after my arrival, I heard from Maurice Oldfield that
he was to take up position as the SIS Liaison Officer in Washington,
and he duly arrived and settled down in a comfortable George-
town house.

We saw each other regularly and I enjoyed both his hospitality
and being mothered by the large black woman who handled the
domestic arrangements of his bachelor establishment.

I visited Maurice frequently, and knew much of what was
going on in the intelligence circles since people in his house spoke
very freely. Sometimes, however, when members of the CIA came
for private meetings in the evening, I would voluntarily leave the
room where they were having discussions and settle myself and my
drink elsewhere until talk on particularly sensitive matters was
over.

I had two friends in Washington from my journalistic days,
General Alfred Gruenther and his wife, whom I had known when
he was at SHAPE and I was based in Paris. The General and his
wife had a formidable reputation as bridge players. I had also
earlier met in Europe James Hagerty, President Eisenhower's press

spokesman, and through Hagerty was able to make my mark with Pierre Salinger, now President Kennedy's press spokesman. Maurice was to establish a close relationship with Kennedy himself and was instrumental in rebuilding the battered reputation of MI6 in America.

It was during President Kennedy's tenure of office that the successful SIS exploitation of a Soviet source enabled the United States to confront the Soviet Union at the brink of a nuclear war and cause Nikita Khrushchev to back down.

From April 1961 and for the next eighteen months, a Russian intelligence officer, Colonel Oleg Penkowsky, passed information to the SIS. It covered a myriad of subjects, but it was intelligence on Soviet missile capability particularly that allowed President Kennedy to act on information which led to his decision to demand that the Russians withdraw missiles being set up in Cuba. During this time, Maurice was constantly discussing with his colleagues at CIA Langley the stream of information produced by Penkowsky.

Penkowsky was a GRU officer working under the cover of the Soviet Committee for Scientific and Technical Coordination. His boss was Dzherman Gvishiani, Premier Kosygin's son-in-law, a charming and distinguished man I was later to meet several times in Vienna.

The son of a White Russian father, Penkowsky decided in about 1958 that he no longer supported the Soviet system, which he felt was more imperialistic and corrupt than the Western democracies appeared to be, so he decided to hasten its downfall by passing high-level intelligence to the West.

Initially Western intelligence did not bite and were obviously suspicious. As an inside agent Penkowsky was too good to be true, and many felt he was a plant. But he persevered and at the end of 1960, at a Canadian reception, he handed a package of secret documents to a Canadian official. The papers were then passed from one of the Canadian Defence Attachés to his opposite number at the British Embassy, who promptly sent the papers through to Century House. It was this information that convinced SIS that Penkowsky was not a plant, for the Soviets would not pass such highly secret information even as a bait. Penkowsky was therefore judged genuine and the air erupted with signals urging development of this potentially remarkable source.

It was the Chief of SIS, Sir Dick White, who personally took the decision that the relationship with Penkowsky should be nurtured, and no one has so far written about the system developed to run Penkowsky as an active and high-level agent.

But Penkowsky was a very different and difficult agent. The approach had come from him and he was a gifted, intelligent and opinionated man who was more aware of the nuances of intelligence than were many of the intelligence officers committed to his case – whether behind the scenes or face to face.

A special section had to be set up to evaluate the enormous amounts of intelligence, both verbal and documentary, that came from him. Much of this information was handed over in Moscow but, at other times as secretary of the Committee of Scientific and Technical Research, Penkowsky was able to travel to Western Europe, and there he was debriefed for hours in specially prepared safe houses.

Penkowsky gave SIS invaluable information about the entire Soviet defence capacity, particularly with regard to its missiles. His association with the *nomenklatura* (mandarin class) in Moscow, and with his father-in-law, a general, also enabled him to give the West guidance on Soviet policy, although he was not privy to strategy at the highest level.

Through discussions about information given by Penkowsky, Maurice moved closer in his relationships in Washington to the White House and to briefings of President Kennedy himself.

The Cuban crisis raged from July to October 1962, and everyone who lived through it has their own memories of that period, just as they do of the day on which Kennedy was assassinated. Maurice became a genuine admirer of Kennedy and forged a link with the President and his closest advisers that would have served both countries well for the rest of Kennedy's presidency, had it not been cut short by his assassination.

Khrushchev's appeal to Kennedy on 26 October 1962 showed that, in the end, reason was to prevail.

We and you ought not now to pull on the ends of the rope in which you have tied the knot of war, because the more the two of us pull the tighter the knot will be tied.

Maurice Oldfield contributed much in his service to Britain, but the feeling of trust in SIS that the CIA redeveloped because of Maurice after the disastrous Philby and George Blake episodes (when that controversial and senior CIA officer, James Angleton, was still reluctant to deal with SIS) was a contribution to world peace.

When I returned to the United States at the end of that week, and went to stay with Maurice, it became clear that he had reached the summit of approval, both from the President himself and CIA. From that time onwards, he told me, he was confident that he would succeed Sir Dick White.

Around this time I made a prolonged trip to Africa, and wrote a detailed account of it at Maurice's request. An edited version of three of the sections appeared in one of America's best newspapers, the *Milwaukee Journal*. The unedited versions were filed for intelligence. One report I wrote concerned Ethiopia, a country so poor when I knew it that it is hard to understand that it became even poorer.

Addis Ababa, Ethiopia, August 1961. The winds of change are blowing strongly against the walls of this historic capital of the kingdom of Solomon and Sheba, and they will bring more progress in the next few months than have the past few centuries.

Ethiopia is best known for its feudal ruler, the King of Kings, Lion of Lions, Conquering Lion of Judah, His Imperial Majesty Haile Selassie Negus Negusti, direct descendant of Solomon and Sheba. Today, the Negus is Ethiopia's greatest claim to fame. And it is on him the winds will wreak the greatest change. Observers are certain the next twelve months will see the overthrow of the archaic despotic ruling system here which despatches political foes by public hanging in the market square.

Considering this is the capital city of a country larger

than Texas with untold natural resources, the poverty and anachronisms of Addis Ababa defy description and are beyond the bounds of most imaginations. Here there is a fantastic combination of splendour and squalor. Outside the city through the rest of the country is mainly squalor.

Halfway up Churchill Road, named after the British Premier who restored the Emperor to his throne after British troops drove out the Italians in World War II, scrawny hyenas scavenge on the site that was to have been the National University, while a mile away the Emperor, ensconced in the luxury of his palace, negotiates treaties with foreign powers, or personally buys mules for his army.

Although there are ministers and a government, real power is still in the hands of the diminutive Emperor, who busies himself with even the smallest items of official business, not only buying supplies for the army but also choosing programs for the radio station.

But although small in stature, the Negus is a big man morally and a strong man physically. He has to be to have held on to power for forty-three years in this backward country, where the law of the jungle still rules.

Haile Selassie first became the power behind the throne after a palace coup in 1917. He survived the bitter civil wars and was crowned Emperor in 1930. And he survived the onslaught of Mussolini's legions and a series of coups after the war, culminating with the most dangerous threat to his power last December.

That plot failed, and its leader, General Mengistu Newaye, was hanged on a specially built gallows in the market square. Standing in the back of a truck in his best uniform the General in a gesture of bravura jumped off the back of it before it drew away, and hanged himself. There were many tears and none of the applause that usually greets a public hanging, and already Newaye is becoming a bigger legend in death than he was in life.

How can anybody believe that the present situation can continue? Ethiopia is ruled by a handful of men and families of high birth who own all the land. About a third of it is owned by the Imperial family, a third by the Coptic church and a third by the nobles. There are hardly any taxes on land and although it is some of the most fertile in the whole world it remains badly worked because the peasants get so little out of it.

The hard-working tenant farmer in the southern province of Sidamo has no incentive to produce more than he needs immediately for his family to subsist, for he is obliged to give up two-thirds of all his harvests to an absentee land-lord.

The percentage of educated Ethiopians can be counted on the fingers of one hand, and these are the people who eventually must support the revolution that will overthrow the palace. Today in Ethiopia they are cautious about speaking to strangers – there are many prisons or remote outposts for banishment – for Ethiopia is a police state. But they have been educated in a large degree outside their own country and have rubbed shoulders and broken bread with the young up-and-coming men from Ghana and Guinea – countries which have recently broken loose from colonial control and where the philosophy of Marxism has taken hold.

Both the 'pink' leader of Ghana, Kwame Nkrumah, and the neutralist Gamal Abdel Nasser of Egypt have sought to inflame the 'thinkers' in Ethiopia to overthrow the monarchy. There is little doubt that one day they will – and that day cannot be so far off.

But at the moment, progress in Ethiopia tends to ebb and flow with the mood of the Emperor. Much of the building in the country, be it of roads, of mansions or of offices, has been done for ceremonial occasions rather than as part of a plan for progress. A boulevard will be opened to coincide with the opening of a building for holding international conferences and visits of foreign dignitaries; the road leading up to the Japanese Embassy became shambolic and was never repaired until a visit of the Japanese Crown Prince took place.

The University site, where those hyenas snuffle through

garbage, has lain desolate for almost twelve years after the Emperor laid the cornerstone. The huge pillars for the gate were erected and then, with no explanation, all work was stopped.

Nearly all the good roads in Ethiopia – and there are not many – are those built by the Italians during their occupation. The Emperor has had money from the World Bank for road building and repairing, but little has been done. Inevitably, this leads to charges of corruption, and this is all fuel to the flame for those who look to a democratic government.

Perhaps, because of the obvious appearance of backwardness in this country, Haile Selassie has imbued his court with more pomp and pageantry than any court in Europe. This is a further trouble spot with the young intelligentsia who have imbued socialistic ideas at universities outside their own country.

All of these irritants to the people are obvious to the visitor to the country. He will see – and smell – the squalor in which the people live, he will see the dirt roads littered with dung and garbage, he will see the children covered in sores, and the old woman with half her face eaten away by syphilis, he will see the beggars and the cripples, and he will see the Emperor's pet lions who eat more meat in a day than most large families see in a week.

Ethiopia is a mountainous country, and the communications are bad. There are seventeen different nationalities, many more varied tribes, and seventy different languages are spoken there.

One bright spot, which will help develop the country, is the well-run airline which is bringing much of Ethiopia closer together (except, of course, few Ethiopians can afford to fly). But Ethiopian Airlines, set up under ICA auspices and organized by TWA, is a slick efficient carrier which has a reputation second to none in Africa.

This is one of the few visible signs of American influence or aid in Ethiopia which benefits the man in the street. While the Soviet Union has given Ethiopia a $100,000,000 low-interest, long-term loan, has built a technical school and an oil refinery, and while communist Yugoslavia virtually manages the economy, there are few outward signs of American help.

However, the air force is being trained by the US, by Great Britain and Sweden, while the army is being trained and equipped by the US and the navy is being trained by Norway. The West Germans are working on a dam project for the Blue Nile together with the US, and the Italians and the Yugoslavs have built other power projects.

The US is building roads, but Russia has built a hospital in the capital, staffed by Russians. Communist Czechoslovakia has contributed $20,000,000 credit for hospital equipment.

Whilst the US is undoubtedly doing a great deal for this country, the plum gifts or assistance which catch the eye of the average Ethiopian are donated by the communist bloc. This is dangerous.

Ethiopia cannot be allowed to turn to communism, yet that is the direction she is bound to take if change follows a successful palace revolution. People who know Iraq cannot but remember the revolution there in 1958 which massacred the royal family and put General Kassem in power. Kassem has gradually led his country out of the Western bloc and into the Soviet orbit. Can that be stopped here?

The leaders of the rebellion last December said they wanted to establish a constitutional monarchy, in which the Emperor would be little more than a figurehead, as the Queen is in England.

They hoped for an orderly transfer of power to the Crown Prince Asfa Wossen, the Emperor's son. The rebels felt that a symbol was needed to unify the different tribes and races, and this would have to be a continuation of the Emperor's line. But they were not prepared to accept the present Emperor who had been accepted as a demi-God, and they do not relish waiting for his natural death although he is already past seventy.

Although the December revolt was localized within the

capital and did not have the support of the great majority of the people, of the army or of the church, it did show both the people and the Emperor that the discrepancies between the proposed liberal state set forth in the new constitution and the corruption and despotism of the present regime are the cause of a discontent which can only grow.

The Emperor has realized this and has made concessions by handing over some of his powers, and he has announced plans for the setting up of a normal civil service system. But this is not enough for the intellectuals and leaders of the liberalizing faction. People who know this country do not believe it is enough to stop a further attempt to remove the Emperor.

That next attempt cannot be far off, and it is likely to be a more bloody and costly effort. It may succeed or it may not, but if it does what will it bring? The pattern of previous revolts points to a left-wing military dictatorship, but a civil war could develop which would be an open invitation for foreign powers to intervene.

Having completed the setting-up of a steel pipe-making plant in the United States at Middletown, Ohio, I returned to live in Germany and then Switzerland for the next three years, while I sought to establish plants in the Middle and Far East.

Returning to Europe in 1961 brought me back into contact with the – at that time, at least internally, famous, but about to become notorious – SIS officer, Kim Philby.

It was well known that probably the finest hotel in the Middle East was the St George's in Beirut; and whenever I travelled to or from the Middle or Far East, I would always break my journey in Beirut and stay there. Soon after my first stay there, I started negotiations with a fine Christian Arab gentleman, Emile Bustani, who had built up the contracting company CAT and who, incidentally, owned the St George's. His partners, Abdulla Khoury and Shukri Shammas, also became my contacts and good friends, and I could not have had better advisers and supporters for business with the whole of the Middle East.

It was Emile Bustani who took me to Kuwait and introduced me to three of the heads of leading Kuwaiti families, Abdulla Al Ghanem, later to become a Kuwaiti minister, Abdul Aziz Al Baher, then Chairman of one of the large Middle East banks which his family controlled, and Hamad Al Hamad, another leading businessman and banker. It was also a pleasure to meet Bader Al Mulla, son of the hereditary Secretary of State of Kuwait and a prominent businessman, who was involved in setting up Annabelle's in London. These gentlemen were the basis on which Bustani and I set about establishing the Kuwait Pipe Company, in which we all took a share, and after that I visited Kuwait probably every other month for the next three years.

CHAPTER 16

IT WAS IN BEIRUT that I met Kim Philby again. During my time in R5 he had been our Liaison Officer in Washington, and when he visited Headquarters in London he invariably visited R5, as he had done before his appointment to Washington.

I thought it worthwhile, during my visits to Beirut in 1962, and before he departed for Moscow in January 1963, to have a drink or ten with him every now and then for old time's sake, if nothing else. Philby frequented either the bars in the Normandy Hotel or the St George's, and was a well-known figure amongst the journalistic community at that time.

My old friend from UP, Larry Collins, was now the Newsweek correspondent, and in Beirut there was always an interesting gathering of intelligent and convivial correspondents.

Philby appeared at his ease among my friends and consumed large quantities of alcohol without it ever seeming to have any effect on him. I invariably met him for a pre-lunch drink which, of course, usually meant I had no lunch; for even by Middle Eastern standards of lunch at 2.30 or 3 p.m., a lunch-time drink with Kim Philby would last well into the afternoon.

Kim Philby's activities have been dealt with by at least a dozen other authors. I must stress that although I met Kim whilst we were both working in SIS, what I know of him results from meetings with him or discussion with others about him since I left SIS.

I cannot remember exactly the day on which I first met him, but it was on the seventh floor of Broadway Buildings, in an office shared by Tony Milne and Sir Gyles Isham. The seventh floor was occupied by R5, Philby's old section into which I was introduced when I started my career in SIS. Douglas Roberts, who had been my boss in SIME when I was in the Middle East, was Head of R5 and Tony Milne was both his senior staff officer and deputy. Gyles Isham, who now had responsibility for studying the Russian intelligence services and their organization in the Soviet Union, I already knew from Palestine. Tony Milne and his brother Tim were both friends of Philby, and it was inevitable that when Philby visited London from Washington he would call in to see them.

Philby had handed over R5 to Douglas Roberts when he took up his position as the SIS Liaison Officer with the CIA and the FBI. Thus, while he represented the whole of the SIS organization in Washington, he was particularly close to R5 as the section responsible for the study of foreign intelligence organizations, and for liaison with friendly services.

Whenever I spoke to Douglas Roberts I accorded him the respect due to a senior officer (in SIS his rank of Head was the equivalent of a General), and whilst – once we were out of the Army, and in SIS – he always used my Christian name, I was punctilious in calling him Sir and phrasing my speech accordingly. Philby was of similar rank in the Service, but when I met him that afternoon in the gloomy office in R5 some time, I think, during 1949, nothing about Kim's presence suggested that I should offer him the deference and respect which I had for Roberts.

I was introduced to him and he shook my hand. As conversation developed it was obvious that he expected to be called Kim, even by junior officers like myself. The conversation was generally about America and the CIA, and I listened attentively for, at this time, I had neither visited the United States nor had had any direct contact with CIA officers. I recall that most of the remarks made by Kim deprecated the way the Agency operated.

It was clear to me that Kim dealt at only the highest level. If any R5 desk officer had a problem which involved contact with the Americans, it was generally passed up to the Head of R5 and handled by Tony Milne, who would work with the local CIA representative, at this particular time Winston Scott. Kim Philby's work, however, was much more of a representation of MI6 policy in Washington, in which he took his instructions either from the Chief or ACSS Jack Easton.

I bumped into Kim again three or four times in London but

was never again involved in as long a conversation with him – while I was still in the Service – as I was on the day I first met him.

From then until the defection of Burgess and MacLean little more was heard about Philby within SIS, and what one did hear related to what position Philby might occupy in the Service after Major General Sir Stewart Menzies eventually retired. (Certainly, amongst thinking officers in the Service, the thought that Menzies's number two, General Sir John Sinclair, might succeed was anathema.)

Between the defection of the two diplomats and the time I left the Service, Philby's position was obviously being considered, but I knew no more of him until I heard that he had left the Service and returned to journalism. There was considerable resistance within SIS from people who knew Philby to accept that he might be a traitor. Only after the disaster of the operation to spy on the Russian cruiser *Ordzhonikidze*, while she was lying in Portsmouth harbour during the visit to Britain of the Soviet leaders Bulganin and Khrushchev, did it come to be believed. It was the *Ordzhonikidze* affair which resulted in Sinclair being replaced by Sir Dick White, then Head of MI5, who in turn was succeeded by his deputy, Roger Hollis. It was White who decided that the link with Philby should be severed.

And so it was, but only in the sense that Kim was no longer a professional intelligence officer of the inner cadre of SIS. He continued to be in touch with SIS on an informal basis, and in September 1956 he arrived in Beirut as the correspondent for the *Observer* and the *Economist*. There he stayed and there I would meet him until he took off for Moscow on 23 January 1963.

The first time I met Kim in Beirut I sought him out at the Hotel Normandy. At that time the Normandy was the thinking man's hotel, and although it ranked some way behind the St George's, it was certainly better than most other hotels.

I had seen Philby very briefly during my stay in Beirut in 1958, and, knowing he was still there, I took a cab one morning in the autumn of 1961 to the Normandy Hotel, where I found Kim drinking with two journalist colleagues: one a distinguished former Army officer with a monocle and the other Ralph Izzard. From then on all four of us met occasionally for a drink or a meal whenever I was in Beirut, but more often than not I met him alone in the opulent bar of the St George's. It seemed that Kim always wanted to talk about SIS matters and personalities and therefore believed I was more likely to be forthcoming about what I knew if there were no witnesses. I talked to him just as I would have talked to any other former colleague from the Secret Service. Kim had been held in such awe by people who I respected, that, while accusations of treachery had already been levelled against him, I believed that if he were still in touch with members of the Service it was right to give him the benefit of the doubt. After all, I too considered myself badly treated by the Service, yet two of its most senior officers, George Young and Maurice Oldfield, continued to be close friends and I knew that I was certainly not a Russian agent. I believed and felt the same situation prevailed with Kim. At that time it was just inconceivable that somebody who had been as important to the Service as Philby could have been a traitor.

CHAPTER 17

MUCH HAS BEEN WRITTEN about the coup which returned the Shah to power and ousted Dr Mohammed Mossadeqh, the Persian Prime Minister, who nationalized the Anglo-Iranian Oil Company in March 1951 – but little of what has been written is accurate.

Dr Mossadeqh was removed through skilful planning by SIS, with some little help from the CIA, although Kermit (Kim) Roosevelt, in his book *Counter Coup* (1979), claimed virtually all the credit.

Although I was still active in the Service when Mossadeqh took over in Iran, I had left by the time he was removed in August 1953. What I write about, therefore, has been gleaned from talking to the people involved, some of whom are friends. In his book *Through the Looking Glass*, Anthony Verrier says:

> The CIA has been given credit for the Shah's return and Mossadeqh's subsequent downfall. One former member of the CIA, Kermit Roosevelt, has even claimed as much in an idiosyncratic version of these events. The truth is that the CIA took little part in the business, except in the final phase and after Washington had decided that a policy of working with Britain to restore the Shah's powers and against Britain to increase America's stake in Middle East oil (they got 40 per cent in the consortium that was subsequently formed) was, indeed, a sound combination of diplomacy and commerce.

It was no secret that the American Embassy was anxious to discredit the British in Iran and that two of their diplomats, Anthony Cuomo and Roy Melburne, actively negotiated with Mossadeqh under the guidance of US Ambassador Loy Henderson.

It was Ambassador O'Grady who had actively encouraged the National Front, led by Dr Mossadeqh, to demand the nationalization of the Iranian oil industry, ostensibly to block any Soviet attempt to secure an oil concession in the Caspian basin.

An American General, Norman Schwarzkopf, who had been the Senior Military Adviser to the Imperial Iranian Gendarmerie, was approached as a possible intermediary to the Shah, because he was known to be in touch with the Shah's twin sister Princess Ashraf, but the coup itself was really engineered by a long-serving British SIS officer who lived in Iran, and who had a close relationship with the Shah and with three Iranian brothers called the Rashidians. With the SIS officer they were known collectively as 'The Brothers'. Radio communication was maintained with SIS Headquarters in Cyprus, at that time under the command of George Young.

It is true to say that although SIS planned the coup for two years, the unpopularity of Mossadeqh's regime combined with the threat that if he went he would be replaced by the Tudeh party, a revolutionary communist party second in age only to the Soviet party, suddenly brought the people on to the streets demanding that Mossadeqh go. But it was the encouragement and persuasion that SIS contrived to arrange for this demonstration, and the help they immediately gave to the Shah's supporters, that returned the Shah – in temporary exile from the capital – in triumph, and ensured Mossadeqh was brought to trial. In view of his age and past distinguished career, Mossadeqh was sentenced to house arrest and spent the rest of his life in his own country mansion, where he wrote his memoirs, published in Tehran at the end of 1986.

The CIA's only contribution to the coup was that, when they saw which way the wind was now blowing, they affixed portraits of the Shah to their cars and drove around Tehran sounding their horns and flashing their headlights. The Americans claimed afterwards they were lending their support to the people rather than to the Shah or to Mossadeqh.

In the purge that followed the ousting of Mossadeqh, it was found that nearly seven hundred officers in key positions in the Military and in J.2 (the forerunner of SAVAK) were members of the military wing of the Communist party.

Dr Hossein Fatemi, the owner and editor of the widely read newspaper *Bakhtar-Emrouz* (*West Today*) who had been installed by Mossadeqh as his Foreign Minister, and who always gave the impression of being an Anglophile was, in fact, a Tudeh party sympathizer and was sentenced to be executed.

In the aftermath of the coup, the Shah received George Young, who had handled the operation from Cyprus, and from then on formed a very close relationship with SIS and its chiefs. The Shah told a close friend of Young that, 'In times of crisis he is a man who can take decisions and throw caution to the winds. Young is a man who believes that friendship cuts two ways and that Britain should stand by her friends even at the risk of offending others.'

After the coup one of the first MI6 Station Heads we appointed to Tehran was Teddy de Haan, with whom I had worked closely in Germany and Austria. The Shah asked that de Haan and subsequent Station Chiefs, such as Alexis Forter, report to him regularly, and the more competent of the MI6 representatives in Tehran soon had more influence with the Shah than the British Ambassadors, which proved an irritant to most Ambassadors.

It is still not generally known that the ceding of the two Tomb islands and the Mussa island in the Persian Gulf (which are of great strategic importance to Iran) followed months of hard bargaining, pressure and negotiations. It was resolved by Lord Home appointing a long-retired expert on the Gulf, Sir William Luce, to oversee them. This resulted in a period of six months when the Shah declined to have any contact with the British Ambassador or his staff, and the only link with the British Government was through an SIS member whom he trusted completely.

When he was Chief, Maurice Oldfield saw the Shah regularly, often meeting in Zurich, and had a close and intimate relationship with His Imperial Majesty. Out of friendship, Maurice promised the Shah that while he was Chief, SIS would not conduct any internal espionage against Iran or have any direct contact with Armed Forces officers or negotiate with the Mullahs. Maurice admitted to me after the fall of the Shah that he had felt obliged to keep the promise for the sake of relations between himself and the Shah, although he did it against his better judgement and regretted it deeply after the ousting of the Shah by Khomeini. This is not the only time that keeping his word cost Maurice dear.

In his book *The Pride and the Fall*, Sir Anthony Parsons, the last British Ambassador to the Shah, who had collected a Military Cross whilst an officer in the Arab Legion, and whom I greatly admire, said he would not have SIS spying on Iran from his Embassy.

The Shah was surrounded by sycophants and there were really only two people who could speak freely to him. One was the long-standing British SIS officer in Tehran and the other was Assadollah Alam, a former Prime Minister, and then Minister of the Court, in which position he really continued to outrank the Prime Minister, Amir Abbas Hoveyda, a diplomat and technocrat. Hoveyda and Parsons were close friends from the days when both had served in their respective embassies in Ankara, while Assadollah had grown up with the Shah, being a playmate of his when they were small boys.

There were many, during the last five years of the Shah's rule, who feared for the future because of the hostile international press that the Shah received.

In 1971 I was approached by Tehran and asked if I would work in Prime Minister Hoveyda's office as an adviser on press matters, but I declined. On reflection I regret the decision.

My experiences in Iran were greatly helped by my SIS friends and connections, and I was later able to arrange a large amount of business with General Toufanian, Head of Arms Procurement and Purchases. The signing of agreements with him and his staff involved regular visits to Tehran between 1972 and 1975. A sadness about Tehran, however, was that one of my friends from my earliest days in journalism, Joe Alex Morris, was killed during the bloodshed which followed Ayatollah Khomeini's return to Iran in 1979. He was representing the *Los Angeles Times* when a stray bullet hit him.

Whenever he is in England I still see the former SIS member and friend of the Shah who contributed so much towards the organization of the coup which pre-empted a possible pro-Soviet coup in 1953, and whose help to Irano-British relations is still immeasurable. He is a modest and humble man who may still have a contribution to make in Iran, but he would only ever act when the interests of Britain coincided with those of the Iranian people. His loyalty to SIS has been rewarded by the highest decoration given to anyone in the Secret Service who has not achieved the rank of CSS.

CHAPTER 18

IN THE SUMMER OF 1965 I decided to move back to England and live in London. We were a family of four now, my French wife Odile and two daughters. It was to our flat in Palace Gate that Maurice Oldfield came on the evening of 16 November 1965, to tell me that he had become ACSS. It was his fiftieth birthday. From then on we met frequently, both to play bridge and – when Maurice wanted – to discuss matters of interest or ways in which I could be of help to him.

I worked from home as a consultant for business and financial matters, and one morning I received a telephone call out of the blue. The caller, who wished to remain anonymous, said he was telephoning from Paris but would like to come over to London to see me. He mentioned the name of a friend I trusted and whom I had seen recently in Rome. We agreed that the caller would visit me at the flat two days later.

At the time suggested the caller presented himself at my front door and – after I had taken his hat and large coat, and coffee had been served – he quickly got to the point. He said that our mutual friend had spoken highly of me and mentioned that I travelled a great deal, particularly in the Middle East. He had come to ask me if I would work for his country's intelligence service. Due to his country's close relationship with the UK, his own service did not operate in this country, but, if I wished confirmation as to who he was and what he offered, I should telephone his country's ambassador or else the military attaché in London. We had a detailed discussion, and then arranged for him to call on me in a week's time to see what my thinking was. Having already half decided to accept, I arranged a meeting with Maurice to tell him of the offer. He was furious. He told me to leave well alone and that he would deal with the matter. It was the last I heard of that particular poaching attempt and I was somewhat disappointed. The intelligence game gets into one's blood and I would have found it stimulating to work with one of the most efficient intelligence services that exists.

I thought at this time that my future might lie in politics and was sufficiently pleased with myself to think that the Central Office of the Conservative Party would welcome me with open arms as a parliamentary candidate. However, I had just written a letter to *The Times*, which was published rather prominently and which convinced the mandarins that I was too controversial and probably too bloody-minded. My parliamentary ambitions thus floated away until I was approached by the Conservative Association in Harlow in 1972, and after two selection committees, I was chosen as their prospective parliamentary candidate, behind the back of and without the blessing of Central Office. At that time Harlow was a left-wing constituency and I knew in advance my efforts were doomed to failure.

Through a meeting on the Cresta Run in St Moritz, I was invited to join William Brandts and Company, a merchant bank and one of the sixteen accepting houses recognized by the Bank of England. From what started as a part-time position of adviser in the International Department, my job changed into being a main Board Director and head of the International Department within six months.

The Chief Executive of Brandts was Michael Andrews whom I considered then and still consider now to have one of the keenest minds in the City.

When I became a merchant banker many old colleagues made remarks about merchant bankers living by their wits. It is traditional that merchant banks put deals together, but rarely put their own money into them. After I had been in the bank for about six months, I was asked, as an outsider, to write a paper for Brandts on the principal distinctions between merchant and commercial banking (put another way, between wholesale and retail banking). At the time Brandts was a subsidiary of Grindlays, and I used the throwaway sentence in my paper, 'The merchant banker is generally the intellectual and social superior of the commercial banker.' Much like the relationship between MI6 and MI5.

Whilst all the merchant bankers I knew agreed with this description, it was not something that went down well with the bankers of our parent company.

A lot of the business that was conducted in my first years of banking involved 'sovereign risk loans', and I was involved in negotiations with East European countries, Iran, the Arab States and the Far East. I travelled a great deal of this time and enjoyed building up the International Department at Brandts which, after three years, was the equal of any in the City.

Early in 1973, when Maurice Oldfield was appointed Chief of the Secret Intelligence Service, I asked him to come and lunch at the Bank with Lord Aldington, the Chairman, and Michael Andrews. It was the day that Jak had done one of his cartoons of Maurice in the *Evening Standard*, and I remember during lunch we sent out for a copy of the paper and laughed about it. By the time Maurice had become Chief, I had recruited three former MI6 operatives to help me track down international business for the Bank; and it was always a great asset for us when travelling abroad to be able to contact a sympathetic soul who would not only be well informed, but who would also almost certainly have a way of contacting whomever it was one needed to meet.

I travelled a great deal during the next three years on behalf of Brandts in Europe and to the Middle and Far East. I was particularly interested in dealing with bankers in Yugoslavia, and was able to arrange some interesting business with the Ljublyanska Banka, the state bank of Slovenia. The bank had as an adviser Bogdan Gorian, later to become a member of the Federal Parliament and to sit on its Foreign Affairs Committee. Gorian arranged some chamois hunting expeditions for me, and I have never enjoyed stalking as much as I did on the several occasions that 'Bogo' arranged for me. An old partisan hero, he relived some of his experiences with me as we climbed through the hills where some thirty-five years before he had harassed the occupying Germans.

In Saudi Arabia, I probably had as good an entrée as possible. I had come to know Kemal Adham, the brother-in-law of King Feisal, and the Head of the Saudi Arabian intelligence service. He is one of the most charming and intelligent men that I have met in the Middle East, and he had immense power while his brother-in-law was King. I used to be taken to him by a former Saudi Air Force General, Hashim Said Hashim, who was very helpful to Brandts. Kemal's deputy was Prince Turki Bin Feisal, who took over as Head of the Service when Kemal retired.

In 1975, however, what I considered to be one of the most enjoyable periods of my life came to an end when Brandts overreached itself in the property boom and had to be bailed out by its shareholders, as a result of which control passed to Citibank, an American bank, one of the largest in the world and certainly the most commercially aggressive. The new broom swept pretty clean and I was one of the old-guard directors invited to leave. (There had, anyway, always been a certain amount of controversy about an outsider like myself who, without banking experience, had been made a main Board Director and a departmental head.)

My departure was a big disappointment to me but I decided I still had something to contribute to banking. So often, both for SIS and as a journalist, I found myself meeting the right person at the right time in the right place.

During my business activities in the Far East in the early 1960s, I had opened a bank account in Singapore with the Hong Kong and Shanghai Bank. Peter Hutson, the accountant at the branch in Singapore, where I opened the account, made a great impression on me as a competent and imaginative executive, and I kept in touch with him as he climbed the ladder within the Bank.

At the time that I left Brandts, he was one of the top three at the Bank's headquarters in Hong Kong, and, when I telephoned him to ask if he thought I could be of any use to his bank, he invited me to fly out to Hong Kong to discuss the matter.

The Bank was moving into merchant banking and they had already established Wardley as their merchant banking arm. When I approached Hutson they were preparing to start a Middle Eastern merchant bank to take advantage of the good connections they already had throughout the Middle East, through their control of the British Bank of the Middle East. Ten days after arriving in Hong Kong, having been interviewed by various members of the Bank, including the Chairman, Michael Sandberg, I returned to the UK as Managing Director of the new Middle Eastern merchant bank, called Wardley Middle East Limited and based in Dubai.

I had renewed many of my Middle Eastern connections while at Brandts, and in Kuwait the Al Bahar (Commercial Bank) and Al Hamad (National Bank) families had agreed to go into a new joint venture bank in Kuwait with Brandts.

I was in touch with the families when I left Brandts, and they said they were prepared to continue negotiating with me on behalf of any new principal that I represented, if the principal was acceptable to them. Certainly the Hong Kong Bank was acceptable: and thus began a series of negotiations in the Middle East which carried on for the next three years.

During my time in Wardley we were involved in several big deals, including raising the money for the Dubai Gas Scheme and the Dubai Aluminium Smelter. These projects brought me into contact with the Ruler and his entourage in Dubai, and I also came to know the Ruler of Ras Al Khiama.

My time with Wardley was up at the end of 1978 and I then returned to England to remarry and start a new family. Elspeth and I were married in 1980. Julius arrived eighteen months later. Two years after him his sister, Charlotte, made up our family group.

CHAPTER 19

I HAVE WATCHED the Secret Intelligence Service grow from when I first heard of it in 1946 to the present day. Nothing has happened to change an opinion I formed many years ago that the ideal duo to run that sophisticated and competent organization during the 1960s would have been George Young as Chief with Maurice Oldfield as his deputy.

Whether or not that might ever have come to pass, I do not know. Philby's treason brought Dick White into MI6 as Chief, and Dick White hung on to the position so long that George Young decided to go into the City and become a merchant banker. With his usual aplomb, George quickly produced a book on merchant banking which is now recommended reading for all those who aspire to a fortune in the City.

The Service, its contacts and its friends, all believed that when Dick White eventually retired Maurice would succeed him. When I joined SIS the Chief was Stewart Menzies, and myth had it that he was the natural son of King Edward VII. Menzies was a typical English gentleman with aristocratic leanings, and his *Who's Who* entry was made up mainly of the orders and decorations he had received from foreign powers. He had also won the DSO and MC in the Life Guards in the First World War. I spoke to him only once, when he came into the office of one of his deputies, Air Commodore Jack Easton, while I was at a meeting there. We all stood up and said, 'Good morning, Sir.' Junior officers who rarely saw the Chief would call him 'Sir', whereas the more senior officers who had to do with him, would call him 'Chief', or 'C' or 'CSS'.

Menzies, who had handled the Ultra[1] success during the war,

[1] Early in 1940, SIS got hold of a German Air Force Enigma coding machine. Developments by the Government communication experts then enabled the British

with which he had endeared himself to Churchill and consolidated his postion as the top intelligence man, was succeeded by General John Sinclair, probably a contender for the title of most incompetent 'C' we have ever had. Sinclair lacked sophistication, finesse and general intellectual equipment. He visited Germany on a week's visit while I was there. Germany at that time was the most important territory in which SIS was operating, and Sinclair was shown most of what we were doing in the way of active operations, technical eavesdropping and the general penetration of Poland, Czechoslovakia and the USSR.

Having seen everything that was to be seen and having talked to innumerable of the station's officers, Sinclair could do no better, as he was being put on to the train at Osnabruck to return to London, than comment that one of the drivers' messes needed 'smartening up'.

Sinclair's stewardship came to a welcome end after the clumsy attempt by an underwater expert to examine in Portsmouth harbour the hull of the Russian cruiser *Ordzhonikidze* which had brought Nikita Khrushchev on his visit to Britain in April 1956.

Sinclair was succeeded by Dick White, who kept the job until 1968, and there was utter consternation within the Service when Sir John Rennie was named Chief in 1968. Maurice was the obvious candidate, despite *The Times*, on 2 October 1981, in its obituary of Rennie, stating confidently that 'no suitable candidate was at that time available from within the Service', which smacks of the misinformation and intrigue Maurice continually had to deal with when he did eventually become 'C'.

There was no official announcement about the changing of the guard in SIS, but the press announced that Rennie would be retiring early (his identity had been disclosed, because his son and daughter-in-law were to be tried for a drugs offence). However, the old D-notice procedure, under which the Government would intimate to a newspaper editor when security matters should not be published, was beginning to creak, and editors were beginning to ignore it.

---

to read highly sensitive German wireless traffic throughout the war. The story is told in *The Ultra Secret* by Group Captain F. Winterbotham. The Ultra machine automatically decoded Enigma messages.

Such was the case when Maurice was appointed as 'C'. Once overseas newspapers had mentioned his appointment, UK papers followed and, in August 1973, one London paper published a full page photograph of Maurice and named him as the new Head of MI6. Maurice was appointed by Prime Minister Edward Heath. However, the major part of Maurice's tenure was under Harold Wilson's Labour Government, and at that time he worked with three Foreign Secretaries, James Callaghan, Anthony Crosland and David Owen, with all of whom he got on very well, and when Callaghan became Prime Minister, the relationship continued. At Maurice's suggestion, Callaghan also gave permission for Maurice to brief the Leader of the Opposition, Margaret Thatcher, and these meetings led to an understanding relationship which continued until Mrs Thatcher, as Prime Minister, visited Maurice on his deathbed during the last days of his life.

The week that Maurice became Chief, I invited him to Brandts for lunch. There were only four of us present; Lord Aldington, Michael Andrews and myself, and our distinguished guest. Thereafter, Maurice often lunched at the Bank with me and with other people of interest, among them former colleagues of his from SIS, now in the City.

When Maurice was knighted he had reached the happiest time of his life, and the sadness was still to come. He had achieved supremacy in the secret world, and public acknowledgement had come with his KCMG. Matters had not yet developed so that his every move became a security problem, and he spent much of his free time staying with friends. We met regularly for meals either in quiet clubs or in London's Chinese or Italian restaurants.

As the time for his retirement from MI6 approached, I could feel that Maurice was not at all happy about handing over. Maurice already knew that the Government were considering appointing an intelligence supremo in the Cabinet offices, and whilst he would have liked to take the job himself, he did not feel this would be fair to his successor in SIS. Maurice had sat in Dick White's shadow for twelve years, and afterwards had virtually run SIS during the Rennie regime, and he thought it would be unfair on his successor if he now hung on in a different guise. But the thought that there might be an intelligence supremo affected his choice and recommendation for his successor.

In the end, Dickie Franks, a 'hawk' in the Service, got the job; although since Maurice's retirement we have had three 'C's, all insiders. I have been told that Franks became irritated because Maurice regularly visited the office after his retirement, principally to clear up his papers, which gave Franks the impression that Maurice was continuing to look over his shoulder.

The next eighteen months were a curious and difficult time in Maurice's life. He had nothing official to do, and he was not sure what he wanted to do. He became a Fellow of All Souls and toyed with the idea of doing research, at first on matters relating to his previous interests in medievalism, and then into the effect of intelligence on between-the-wars diplomacy.

It is not harsh or untrue to say that Maurice was like a fish out of water. Having been involved in high-level intelligence for thirty-five years, where his brain was active on intelligence problems during all his waking hours, he was at a loose end, and it affected him no end. He regarded the intelligence work he had done as having been of value to his country, and thus to humanity; for he was a very human man, much concerned with people, and especially those worse off than himself.

His pleasures were often simple. He enjoyed eating and drinking and I used to entertain him regularly in the Savoy Grill.

During those eighteen months in limbo I saw Maurice frequently. In October 1979 I had arranged a lunch for Maurice and Julian Amery at a restaurant in West Halkin Street. I gave Maurice a lift to the restaurant, and, as we waited for Julian, Maurice told me that the Prime Minister had offered him a new job. From what he said, I knew that it was either to do with Rhodesia or Ulster, and I asked him if he was going to accept it, and, if he did, if he could find a use for me. The matter was only touched on briefly during our lunch with Julian, and the following Monday I drove Maurice to the Ulster Office on the corner of Birdcage Walk, where he went in to give his acceptance of the post of Security Supremo for Northern Ireland. As agreed, I did not wait for him. I was rarely to see Maurice again without either a bodyguard or a whole posse of bodyguards in attendance or in the background, until he was in hospital stricken with cancer.

That evening the main television channels highlighted Maurice's appointment in their news bulletins, and I did not hear from him again for nearly a month, when he wanted to come and stay.

From the moment he took up his job in Northern Ireland, he was a prime IRA target and thus felt disinclined to spend weekends either at his home in Derbyshire, or at his flat in Marsham Court. With regard to Derbyshire, he told me sadly, 'I do not want to attract the lightning,' and I believe he found Marsham Court excessively lonely. He badly wanted company and a place where he could relax. He used to wander around the grounds of our house accompanied by our two labradors, Abdullah and Sami. One of my bonds with Maurice was our time together in the Middle East, where we both learnt some Arabic and through which we had both established particular ties. The names of the dogs were a permanent reminder of those days. When Maurice was dying in the King Edward VIIth Hospital for Officers, he asked me to bring him a photograph of my dog Abdullah and it was the sole photograph in Maurice's room when he died.

When Maurice came for the weekend he would arrive in his Government Rover, which bristled with antennae, and accompanied by his two Special Branch bodyguards. They would take a turn about my grounds and then, having arranged a time when Maurice would be collected, would leave him with the general understanding that Maurice would not stir from my house without advising Special Branch by telephone. However, once on our own, Maurice would immediately ask me to drive him to one of the local pubs, and there he would try to forget the responsibilities and worries that weighed on him over pints of beer.

One weekend when Maurice flew in from Ireland, I saw a young man hanging over the gates at the end of my drive, showing excessive interest in my house. I mentioned it to the senior Special Branch officer, but when he went to look, the man had moved on.

The two Special Branch chaps immediately jumped into their car and quickly found the fellow looking over our back gate. When questioned, he claimed to be a student from an Irish university, who once had a girlfriend who had lived in the house, and he just wanted to have a look. This was patently such rubbish that the bodyguard became alarmed and felt Maurice should not be left unattended that weekend. Our house was turned into a fortress. The two Special Branch officers took over the nanny's flat, and uniformed police wearing berets and carrying automatic pistols patrolled the grounds for that weekend, which was anything but peaceful.

During the spring of 1980 it became very obvious to me that Maurice was deeply unhappy and seriously ill. During lunch with my wife and me, he had to leave the table in the middle of the main course and was unable to eat anything afterwards. He was smoking more and his normal consumption of whisky had gone up. He was also losing weight, particularly around his neck. His collars had become too large for him. My mother had died of cancer and I thought I knew the signs. I was convinced Maurice had cancer; and so was Elspeth, who had been a sister at King Edward VIIth Hospital, where Maurice was to die. Maurice admitted that he was ill and said he was being treated by the Civil Service doctors in Ireland, and that he had a consultation with the Treasury doctor in London. The preliminary diagnosis was that he was suffering from diverticulitis. The later diagnosis was an inflammatory condition of the bowel. On 12 June it was announced that his resignation for reasons of ill health had been accepted.

The day after Maurice resigned from his post in Northern Ireland he telephoned me and begged me to come and see him at his flat in Marsham Court. I was appalled at what I found when I got there. At its best his flat was dark, and I had arrived in the evening after the sun had gone down.

Maurice had no lights on at all in the flat and his sitting room was thick with smoke. His ashtray was full of the butts of those horrible cheap cigarillos he smoked, and an almost empty bottle of whisky was by his empty glass on a coffee table.

'For Christ's sake, what *is* the matter?' I asked. He signalled me to sit down while he poured me a whisky and another for himself.

'Tony, I have been lying about my positive vetting.' He said it bleakly, and added, 'I have just resigned.' I looked at him and saw an old and sick man, sick with sadness and with the cancer eating away inside him.

'I have never before contemplated suicide,' he said. 'But I am now, and I need to talk to you.'

Slowly, with the help of another drink, he then told me that every time positive vetting had homed in on homosexuality, he denied ever having had any homosexual experiences. Those he had had went back to his youth before the war.

I assured him that, in his case, I would have done the same. Today, when I consider the number of homosexuals I knew in SIS, it is clear that they had too.

The man who was my boss in Vienna and who eventually led to my downfall, stayed on in the Service until he retired and when he went to take leave of Maurice, who was then Chief, said to him, *apropos* homosexuality, 'Ah, you never knew did you?'

Incredible, since I had known from the moment I met him in Vienna and had always assumed that Maurice had too.

Maurice told me in detail how, as a result of black propaganda concerning allegations in Ulster and Southern Ireland, one of the Fleet Street dailies had taken to keeping his flat under surveillance and had been questioning the porters.

He thought it possible that the fact that he had lied and had admitted to lying could be about to become known and would embarrass Margaret Thatcher, who had appointed him to Northern Ireland and for whom he had great respect. He had therefore had no alternative but to go to Sir Robert Armstrong, the Cabinet Secretary and the PM's unofficial adviser on security matters, admit the whole matter and resign. Maurice told me then and there that the only other person he had discussed it with was Victor Rothschild.

Certain questions obviously stand out. Maurice was brilliant at his job, he loved it and he lived for it. He steered the Service through a difficult period. From the time that he became a senior officer in MI6, it was clear to him – as to everyone else – that it was in his grasp to become Chief.

Unlike George Young, the Deputy Chief, who got sick of

waiting for Sir Dick White to retire and went off into a new field, Maurice waited and continued to hope even when he was inexplicably passed over, and Sir John Rennie was brought in from outside.

Maurice was a deeply religious and moral man and knew in his own heart what sort of a person he was. But he knew he was *not* of the Establishment even though he was within it, and he knew that he would be judged by the Establishment. He decided early that he would not let his 'youthful peccadilloes' stand in the way of his sure accession to the job for which he was undoubtedly the best qualified, the most experienced and – as events proved – the most able.

I have said earlier that there were a large number of homosexuals in MI6: certainly more in MI6 than in MI5. The MI6 man is in general more sophisticated, more urbane and more intelligent than his MI5 opposite number. It is the sort of job which requires total dedication and makes heavy demands on traditional family life and it is this which tends to encourage celibates and homosexuals: indeed, there is a Freudian theory which links such people with a desire for the amassing of information and the complexities and simplicities of state service.

I believe there comes a time when it is too late to confess. Obviously Maurice thought this way, and until the time he went to Washington he could probably have got away with it: confessed and stayed. After that he was marked for greatness, and anyway he had already taken the polygraph test in the United States. American intelligence, in the 1960s, became worried that Maurice was not married, so Maurice volunteered to take a lie detector test, did so and passed – much to their embarrassment at having asked him.

Certainly the KGB has gained out of the recent publicity, and the intelligence services have, yet again, been made to look lacking. But where the matter all started is important, almost more important than the damage it did. An intensive smear campaign was launched in Northern Ireland as soon as Maurice's appointment was known. The allegations – which it has been said originally came from MI5 – were reported back by RUC Special Branch to the Metropolitan Police, which compiled a report for the Commissioner, Sir David McNee. I was aware that a Scotland Yard file linked Maurice with the allegations. A Scotland Yard man leaked the existence of the file to a Fleet Street editor over an informal drink. It was this which resulted in reporters harassing Maurice, into the state in which I found him that evening.

I have already recalled my first memorable meeting with Maurice, and I doubt if there was a scruffier lieutenant colonel in the Army in Egypt. We both had a friend, also a lieutenant colonel, whom we knew to be a homosexual. This colonel was possibly the smartest officer in our Headquarters, if not in all Egypt. His immaculately tailored shorts, socks turned down an additional half an inch to show more of the bronzed leg, highly polished shoes, burnished pip and crown on each shoulder of his tailor-made bush shirt, were a great contrast with Maurice's tatty Other Ranks issue which fitted where it touched.

When I first met him, Maurice was thirty-one. If he was indeed a compulsive homosexual, as claimed, this would have been his peak period. I was an inexperienced nineteen-year-old junior officer. We became friends and between assignments spent quite a lot of time together. Never did I or any other person there receive any indication that Maurice was 'queer'. Of the eight or so officers in SIME at that time, all of us were bachelors, and our ages ranged from nineteen to thirty-five.

Whenever we could, we took out what attractive and unattached English women were available, either from the Women's Services or attached to GHQ (where MI5 secretaries were sent out from London) or locally-employed secretaries, generally daughters of long-time British residents. Without doubt the most beautiful girl we all knew, and possibly the most beautiful girl in Cairo, was our Brigadier's PA. Whenever time allowed, Maurice took her out. We also had a glamorous ATS sergeant whom Maurice escorted from time to time, and who eventually married one of Maurice's officers.

Maurice and I met again when I was recruited by him into MI6 in 1948. We both considered ourselves pretty impoverished. My starting salary was £400 a year and Maurice was on something like £1500, nothing when compared to the standards we had enjoyed in the Middle East. Generally speaking, Maurice paid the drinks bills because, as he said, he had more. Looking back, I suppose, we would probably spend one or two evenings a week together. At this time Maurice was lodging with an old University friend and his wife in Highgate and I had digs off High Street, Kensington.

From time to time Maurice would invite me to visit his home for the weekend at Over Haddon in Derbyshire, close to the Chatsworth estate. Maurice was one of an enormous farming family and, on one occasion, when everyone was at home and the house was full, his mother told me they were short of room and I would have to share a double bed with Maurice. If it had ever passed through my mind that Maurice might have had homo-sexual tendencies, this episode would certainly have crystallized them. Yet Maurice kept to his side of the large bed and I to mine. There was not the slightest flicker of interest on his part.

Later, for a while, our paths tended to separate, for he was in the Far East when I was in Berlin and Vienna. But from the time that he arrived in the United States in the early 1960s, we saw each other regularly from then until he died.

Living in London in the late 1960s, my French wife Odile and I played bridge regularly with Maurice, one fourth being a French friend of Odile, a married woman, who was much taken with Maurice.

Odile had been a fashion model for Christian Dior in Paris and her photograph was often on the cover of European magazines.

'The whole world of French fashion is full of pederasts,' she said recently. 'If I cannot tell one, who can? In all the time that I knew Maurice there was no question of his being one.'

Maurice spent holidays in the South of France with Odile, and Nathalie and Anne, and myself, and was much loved by my parents-in-law. None of these people ever thought there was anything odd about Maurice.

My present wife Elspeth maintains that she, like many women, can recognize certain homosexuals by the way they dress and the way they keep their flat or house. On these two counts, Maurice certainly did not appear to her to be homosexual.

During our long walks in the country, conversation with

Maurice would sometimes touch on sex. We discussed those brief affairs Maurice had or was having with women, and occasionally he would ask me about some of the women I had known, women who were friends of us both. He asked me once whether I had ever had any homosexual adventures and I admitted that I remembered one occasion with other boys in a shepherd's hut in the Swiss mountains as a child. Maurice just nodded.

Maurice worried constantly that he was unmarried. He said it made him a natural target for black propaganda. He said once – half seriously – that life would be so much easier and more pleasant if I could find a wife for him, because work meant that he just did not have the time to devote to that sort of pursuit.

It is well known that the Oldfield family were from fairly humble farming stock, and Maurice sadly told me once that it concerned him that the sort of woman he wanted as a wife might find his family beneath her. He loved his family dearly.

Chapman Pincher wrote in his book, *Traitors – The Labyrinths of Treason*, that the reason Maurice never married was because he suffered from psoriasis. Another Pincher fiction. Pincher also says that it was the Scotland Yard officers assigned to protect Maurice who discovered he was a homosexual. Utterly untrue, as I was assured when I lunched at Scotland Yard on Friday, 24 April 1987, with the specific intent of clearing up certain points in my mind.

The book claims, 'His clearly compulsive homosexuality came to official notice after the Yard assumed responsibility for his protection in 1978.' It is a matter of fact that Maurice was not offered the job in Northern Ireland until October 1979. He had no Scotland Yard protection in 1978. When he did receive protection he had three Special Branch officers, all of whom were known to me. None of them submitted any report relating to his homosexuality and I have been assured that none of them 'while alone in Oldfield's flat ... found books and magazines on sexual perversion and photographs of nude young men', as Pincher claims.

Pincher also states that, while Head of MI6, Maurice was regularly visited at his flat by people of various nationalities including waiters, and that one night he had come in appearing to have been beaten up.

His MI6 bodyguard denies to this day that he ever saw Maurice in a state indicating he had been assaulted. During the whole of his time as Head of MI6, Maurice's flat was bugged for security purposes. Friends of his, such as myself, knew his flat was bugged, and so did Maurice, who approved it. It would have been suicidal for Maurice to have carried on 'homosexual activity', to be recorded on tape or listened into by duty officers at Century House. Had Maurice switched off the bug this would have caused comment, and particularly if it had happened regularly.

Conspiracy theories aside, there was nothing odd about waiters coming and going to Maurice's flat. Brilliant though he was, he could barely fry an egg or boil water, and the majority of his meals were sent for from nearby restaurants.

Still, as Pincher said to me at a party four years ago, 'I have to look after my old age.'

Obviously Maurice might have been wiser in his choice of friends, and he might have been wiser in the way he found time for the young men of different nationalities with whom he came into contact. Peter Wright describes Maurice as being 'lonely'. True – but he did not have homosexual relationships with those he befriended, and friends who knew him well know this to be so.

After the New Year of 1987, my wife Elspeth and I decided to have a couple of days' relaxation. So we went up to Derbyshire and saw Maurice's family – particularly his sister Rene – and also Edmond Urquhart, the padre who had buried Maurice and who had christened my son Julius and my daughter Charlotte. We decided that over Easter I would come up with the family and Julius could learn to fish on the Derwent.

Julius caught his first brown trout the day that a journalist telephoned to warn me that the filth about Maurice would appear in the next day's *Mail on Sunday*.

I immediately telephoned my contact in MI6, and it appeared that the Secret Intelligence Service was unaware of the welter of lies and distortions about to be released on to an unsuspecting and mystified public. I also got on to Edmond and arranged for him to go to see Rene and warn her that there would be some unpleasantness next day.

On that Sunday, with the Service's blessing, I got up at five in the morning and drove down to Bakewell to buy copies of the *Mail on Sunday*, so that the family would learn through me what was happening, not through some hard-nosed reporter ringing up with insensitive questions.

MI6 decided it owed it to Maurice's family to send someone up to advise them of Mrs Thatcher's written statement in the House of Commons on 23 April, which begged more questions than it answered.

CHAPTER 20

FROM MY FIRST MEMORABLE MEETING with Maurice Oldfield in June 1946, until I last saw him in hospital just before he died in 1981, I never saw him lose his temper. There was always something of the Chinese mandarin, or perhaps the Buddhist, about him, in that he was always calm, always tranquil and in complete control of himself. Perhaps this was self-discipline but I prefer to believe that, although in pursuit of his duty to his country he could be cynical and ruthless, he was basically a good person. It was his very strong religious belief which overshadowed everything else in his character. I think at various times in his life Maurice was drawn towards Roman Catholicism.

Maurice was always a generous man, not only materially but also in his treatment of subordinates, whether in the Army or afterwards in SIS. He would not call a driver over a weekend if he needed transport, but would make do with a taxi or public transport. I can remember travelling up to Heliopolis in uniform with him in a Cairo bus, in order to save a staff-car driver giving up part of his rest period. Similarly, Maurice would decode a message himself rather than calling in a girl *codist* who was out at a dinner. When he had a bodyguard at the end of his career, Maurice would try to arrange his social life so that the Special Branch man involved was not kept away from his family at a weekend.

He was inscrutable. Even when particularly damaging news about an operation arrived, and whilst I knew from his conversations afterwards the torment which he went through in taking decisions which put people's lives at risk, he did not show it at the time.

He was modest, even humble. He never forgot or was ashamed of his origins in the farmlands of Derbyshire, and though he consorted with Kings and Prime Ministers, he never forgot that he knew how to get his hands dirty in a farmyard. He loved and was devoted to his family, and never forgave himself for being away in South America when his father died. He was the executor of my will and although he always said he would die before me, he insisted on discussing any wishes I might have, and he took very seriously all such duties which friends thrust upon him. He was best man when I married Odile, and again when I married Elspeth.

With regard to women, Maurice was a charmer. He was delighted that the two ladies became friends. Although Maurice would have liked to have been married, perhaps the greatest problem he needed to overcome was that he was already obsessively wedded to his work. However, when he was with women with whom he could relax (and I certainly found this in my own house, whether with my wife or with female friends), his conversation, both intellectual and anecdotal, held them spellbound. He took Elspeth around the churches in our neighbourhood, and was able to hold forth in such detail about church history from the present right back to medieval times, that any outing with him was awaited by her with pleasure.

He delighted in good food and wine, and in the company of two or three close friends a large amount of whisky would always be consumed over the exchange of cleverly-spun stories.

A wide range of stories have finally surfaced about the bitterness of the intrigues and internal rivalry within the intelligence services, particularly in relation to MI5 and Prime Minister Harold Wilson and his eventual resignation as leader of his party. These revelations have been developed further in Peter Wright's book, *Spycatcher*.

I have been told by a senior intelligence officer that Harold Wilson proposed to Oldfield that MI6 should investigate allegations of a 'coup' being organized by right-wing MI5 officers and South African intelligence, and then reveal its existence.

I was told that Maurice said to Wilson, 'You have the wrong man in me, Prime Minister,' and subsequently reported the matter to James Callaghan.

It was always clear to me from things he said that Maurice was somehow involved in the sudden resignation of Harold Wilson from the premiership. I also linked to this the fact that on Maurice's retirement from MI6, the new Prime Minister recommended him for an advancement in the Order of St Michael and St George. The Queen awarded him the Grand Cross of that Order, and he was the first and so far the only Chief of MI6 to be so honoured.

It is true that it was to Maurice that Peter Wright, the MI5 man, went in the summer of 1975 with his report on an MI5 plan to destabilize the Wilson Government. And it was Maurice who told Wright to report it to his own superiors: advice that angered rather than pleased MI5, and did nothing to ease Maurice's burden when he later took on the post of Northern Ireland supremo over the heads of MI5.

Maurice always insisted to me that Harold Wilson, after his retirement, was at great pains to avoid him. Since Wilson lived in Lord North Street and Maurice in Marsham Court, they were almost neighbours, and Maurice said that Wilson would always cross the street if he saw Oldfield coming. Similarly, if they both appeared at the same gathering, Wilson would make every effort not to be near or even in the same room as Maurice.

Baroness Falkender, who, as Marcia Williams, worked closely with Wilson, both when he was in and out of office, has suggested that as Wilson did not see very well, he would not be aware that Oldfield was in his vicinity.

While I believe her when she rubbishes various smears that have been put about as to why Wilson retired, and insists that Wilson had made it known when he returned to Downing Street for the last time that he intended to retire before the end of the parliament, I believe there was something that triggered Wilson's abrupt resignation, and it is related to something about which no outsider knows all the details.

Wilson travelled a great deal, both when in and out of office and particularly to Warsaw Pact countries. This may be one of the facts which so worried MI5.

One is forced to ask, therefore, what action the KGB would take if they had evidence of some theoretical indiscretion on the part of a British Prime Minister.

They would not consider approaching the PM directly or

indirectly. What the KGB would probably do, therefore, is to pass what they had to the CIA or to MI6, secure in the knowledge that it would cause chaos. It would make little difference who received it, since the CIA distrusted Wilson and would certainly pass anything on to MI6, though whether they would be explicit about the source of the material is another matter.

Be that as it may, if something came into Maurice's hands relating to the Prime Minister of the day, his duty would be clear. He would show it to one of three people: the Prime Minister himself, the Cabinet Secretary or his immediate boss, the Foreign Secretary. I believe from things Maurice said that something may have come into his hands and that he showed it to the Foreign Secretary, James Callaghan.

That this coincided with the culmination of a long-standing MI5 campaign to discredit the Prime Minister – a campaign originally fired by a CIA theory based on evidence from Golitsin, a discredited defector – merely served to increase Wilson's distaste for intelligence matters and intelligence people in general.

Maurice did tell me, however, that he had to admit to the Prime Minister that there was 'a section of MI5 which was unreliable'. Whether or not MI5 were tied in to the PM's resignation, weird and disturbing things were undoubtedly happening within MI5 at this time, particularly in Northern Ireland, and there is no doubt that the serious campaign against Oldfield was started there.

A story was 'leaked' in Belfast about Maurice's resignation and was picked up by the *Sunday Times* of 26 April 1987, alleging that Maurice had travelled alone to a pub in Ulster over one weekend and drank there alone, unrecognized, throughout the afternoon. The allegation went on that while the worse for drink he had followed a man into the gentlemen's lavatory and propositioned him. The resulting complaint from the man was supposed to have initiated the enquiries into Maurice's behaviour.

Subsequent investigations have shown that the pub supposedly involved was one regularly used by the RUC – who would have recognized him – which was about twenty miles from Stormont. As Maurice did not drive, it is difficult to imagine that he hitch-hiked undetected to the pub; and certainly when I saw him in

Ulster, he always had two car loads of bodyguards with him. Recent enquiries at the pub, which is now closed, have shown that nobody from the manager downwards can remember anything about this incident.

The black propaganda campaign against Maurice started in 1972, increased the year later when he became Chief of MI6 and was reinforced with a vengeance in 1979 when it became known that he was to be the new Security Supremo for Northern Ireland. It continues today.

I had discussed Northern Ireland with Maurice before he went there, and it was quite obvious to me that he would bring something to that problem which was new. He was a Whitehall servant with immense authority, who understood the working of the Catholic mind and who could argue the theological pattern with any Roman Catholic cleric. There is little doubt that the sudden influx of 'supergrasses' from the IRA was due mainly to Maurice's behind-the-scenes work with the Roman Catholic priests.

Maurice Oldfield's special study during his post-graduate work at Manchester University had been medieval history: he was also intensely interested in Judaism and Roman Catholicism. It quickly became clear to me that he was the first man from Whitehall to hold power who could argue religion with any Catholic priest on equal terms. This was well known to his intelligence 'colleagues' in MI5 and those services working with them: Colin Wallace, a former Army intelligence officer, has confirmed to me that the black propaganda was started as soon as Oldfield was known to be involved in Ireland.

Once Oldfield arrived at Stormont with the innocuous title of Security Coordinator, the anti-Oldfield propaganda increased and was picked up by the Southern Irish press and by the underground press in Britain. Oldfield meanwhile made direct contact with certain leading Roman Catholics and attended off-the-record meetings with various priests, whom he was able to persuade to help him in intelligence gathering in an attempt to break the circle of sectarian violence and political deadlock.

This caused Maurice many enemies, although it would appear there were soon more to be found amongst the Protestant ultra right-wing than amongst the Catholics. It was these, Maurice said, he found just as sinister, if not more so, than those of the IRA. In his early days in hospital, Maurice began to say more than half seriously that he had been poisoned during his stay in Ireland. He told me he found it incredible that while he was slowly dying of cancer, this was not diagnosed until it was too late to save him.

CHAPTER 21

IN 1978, BARRIE PENROSE and Roger Courtier published a book called *The Pencourt File*. Two months after the Prime Minister resigned, these two investigative journalists had been summoned to his home by Harold Wilson. He told them, amongst other things, that he suspected the loyalty of certain senior MI5 officers and that he was convinced that his telephone had been bugged by MI5. He had consulted both Maurice as Chief of MI6 and Sir Michael Hanley as Head of MI5 and had been told that MI5 contained a 'disaffected' faction.

It was extraordinary that a former Prime Minister should be accusing what had been his own primary security organization of the state of working against him, but after a brief flurry of interest in the media the whole matter was supposedly forgotten.

Even though Penrose was sure there was at least some substance to the accusations, little else happened and everything was damped down until a furore was caused by the Government's clumsily-handled attempts to suppress a book by a former MI5 officer, Peter Wright. Wright stated in Australia that MI5, or a section of MI5 orchestrated by him, had broken the law while actively working to discredit not only Wilson and the Labour Government, but also the preceding Conservative Prime Minister, Edward Heath.

In the *Sunday Times* on 22 March 1987 Penrose led the front page with the headline, MI5 'PLOTTED' ULSTER STRIKE. The source of Penrose's story was a former MI5 agent, James Miller. Miller's claims are supported by two former British Army intelligence officers, Colin Wallace and Fred Holroyd; both of whom worked in Northern Ireland, and are now themselves victims of a campaign of disinformation.

I have met both Wallace and Holroyd, and have to confess that the story they tell is frightening and disquieting, but one which ties in with many events to which I have been privy over the past ten years. What has caused me to give credence to these statements is the fact that Wallace asserts that Sir Maurice Oldfield while Security Supremo was also the target for a black propaganda campaign. Details of this campaign match closely details which were told to me privately by Maurice.

In 1971 Edward Heath, who was then Prime Minister, called on Sir John Rennie, at that time Chief of SIS, to take part in the intelligence effort in Northern Ireland. Since Rennie, a former diplomat, had little practical experience of intelligence work, the matter was dealt with by his deputy, Maurice. From that moment on, Northern Ireland figured large in Maurice's life and eventually killed him. Shortly afterwards Maurice succeeded Rennie as 'C', and in 1979, he was recalled from retirement by Prime Minister Margaret Thatcher and sent to Northern Ireland as Intelligence Supremo.

MI5 were bitterly jealous of MI6's move into Ulster, since they believed that Northern Ireland was clearly their territory as part of the United Kingdom, and information which is now emerging seems to confirm that MI5 took active steps to 'sabotage' the work of SIS.

Colin Wallace, who has confirmed this information to me personally, puts it as follows:

The 1973–4 period was particularly critical because it was, in my opinion, a watershed in the battle for supremacy between MI5 and MI6. In the UK the problems associated with the increases in international terrorism, the miners' strike, the three-day week, and alleged increases in the power and influence by left-wing activists all had a profound effect on the roles of the two services.

In Northern Ireland the chief intelligence post was given to an MI5 officer, Dennis Payne, much to the chagrin of SIS. As you can imagine, Ireland was, at that time, the 'in' place to be both in military and intelligence terms. If one examines most of the top posts held in these fields today, the incumbents have, almost without exception, had experience in Northern Ireland.

There was a strong difference of opinion between MI5 and SIS over who should have overall responsibility for the 'Irish problem' – particularly in the case of operations in the Republic of Ireland. To make matters worse, the two services regarded Army Intelligence as amateurs and the RUC Special Branch as totally unreliable. You can imagine the problems such a situation created for joint operations and channels of reporting.

In theory the head of Army Intelligence in the Province was a full Colonel, Peter Goss, who came under the direction of MI5's Dennis Payne. SIS, who came under the direction of Payne, had their own senior officer at Army HQ at Lisburn, Craig Smellie, and a complete office at Laneside, and reported directly to Century House.

When MI5 gained control of the overall intelligence operation they tried to replace those who were already in key posts with others with total loyalty to them. For example, in 1974 there was an attempt to use SAS personnel to replace the Army's normal Special Military Intelligence Unit men. This was a total disaster. Not only did MI5 have much less experience in running agents in a hostile environment than SIS, the SAS at that time had no experience of Northern Ireland-type operations – they had been prohibited from taking an active part (officially at least) for purely political reasons. After a number of quite amazing blunders, the SAS were withdrawn from plainclothes duty in the Province. As the hostility between the various intelligence factions increased they began to 'nobble' each other's operations. The Army had a number of key agents 'taken out' by the terrorists and a FINCO [Field Intelligence NCO] in Belfast committed suicide.

It became quite clear that MI5 were trying to get the SIS removed from the Province completely – this they almost achieved by late 1976.

In Maurice's view it was undoubtedly the pressure of increasing in-house rivalries and the danger it was causing which caused Mrs Thatcher to ask him to come out of retirement and reorganize from scratch the whole intelligence empire in Northern Ireland.

Smear campaigns were being organized against anybody of consequence who appeared to be sympathetic to the position of the Catholic minority in Ulster, or who showed that he believed in a settlement based on radical changes in the Northern–Southern Irish relationship. Among those targeted were Edward Heath, Harold Wilson, Edward Short, roughly twenty other MPs and also the first Catholic Chief Constable of the RUC (from 1973 to 1976), James Flanagan.

The smear campaign against Oldfield was started before he even arrived in Ireland, and Wallace insists that MI5 officers were behind it.

In his biography of Oldfield, Richard Deacon says that Oldfield was becoming increasingly worried and dismayed by a whispering campaign against him. 'Somebody obviously wanted him removed from Belfast,' Deacon says. He also quotes Mrs Elizabeth Roberts, the wife of our former Brigadier and a friend of both Oldfield and myself, to whom Oldfield had said, 'If they don't get me one way, they'll get me another.'

Not only was the smear campaign wearing Oldfield down, this was also the time that he became extremely ill. He had gone to Northern Ireland a reasonably fit man and when he started having stomach problems he saw the Government medical authorities in Ulster, and was told he had diverticulitis.

I saw him often between his resignation and the day he died. We gave a pre-Christmas lunch party on 14 December 1980, and many old friends, intelligence or otherwise, many of them much older than Maurice, made the effort to travel down to see him – including Sir Robin Brook, Commander Antony Courtney, Sir Kenneth Newman, Sir Ian Hogg and George Young, to name a few of the sixty who were there.

Maurice sat for most of the pre-lunch drinks, and everybody who commented on his health – and most did – said to me that he looked seriously unwell.

So it was that early in 1981, when Maurice was due to stay

with us for a weekend, he rang on the Saturday morning and said he did not feel up to coming. I asked him if he had seen a doctor and he said no, he did not want to bother anybody over a weekend. I said that this was quite ridiculous and promptly rang a doctor well known to SIS who was a friend to both Maurice and myself. The doctor went to see Maurice and straight away was certain that he was dealing with a case of cancer. Maurice was immediately put into the King Edward VIIth Hospital for Officers, where he died on 11 March 1981.

EPILOGUE

At about 6 o'clock in the morning of that day, my bedside telephone rang and my doctor friend told me that Maurice had died early that morning. I immediately thought I should go up and check what papers there had been in his hospital room. I did so, and passed on various things to his sisters who were at the hospital. I recovered the photograph of my dog Abdullah, which still hangs in our sitting room.

Several times during his last few months Oldfield said to me, 'I wonder if they are trying to poison me.' He never specified the 'they', and I always assumed he meant the IRA. We discussed whether he might have been poisoned, and I always discounted it.

However, Peter Wright in his book on intelligence says, 'MI5 took part in discussions at the Government's Porton Down Research Centre [the germ warfare research station] to produce a poison which would be untraceable in "assassination operations" overseas.' It has been suggested that 'overseas' included Northern Ireland. It was also Peter Wright who went to Porton Down to enquire whether Hugh Gaitskell, the Labour leader prior to Harold Wilson, could have been poisoned by the KGB rather than dying from Lupus Disseminate.

Maurice died in King Edward VII's Hospital for Officers where he was in the care of Sir Richard Bayliss – Head of the Queen's Medical Household.

I asked Bayliss if he believed Oldfield could have been poisoned.

Bayliss said that Maurice was killed by cancer of the stomach and he knew of no poison which could have caused this. He did, however, say he found it difficult to understand how it was that, for nine months prior to Maurice entering King Edward's where he came under Bayliss's care, his illness should have been diagnosed as diverticulitis.

APPENDIX I

Internal SIS Circular

SIR MAURICE OLDFIELD

You will have seen accounts of the statement made by the Prime Minister today about Sir Maurice Oldfield.

An event like this, with all the innuendo and ill-informed press comment which accompanies it, is bound to be a shock to all of us. Those who served with Maurice will feel dismay and concern and sadness, particularly those who knew him well.

It is perhaps important and of some comfort to separate the personal aspects from the wider professional considerations. As the Prime Minister indicated, the facts became known after Maurice left the Service, and his PV certificate was then withdrawn. There is no evidence that the security of our work was in any way prejudiced, of which the best confirmation is that during his period in office the Service's record of achievement was very high. That record and your own contributions to it still stand, and we can all be proud of them. It is this that we must remember during these difficult days. The fundamental integrity of the Service remains intact, and our determination to continue to perform our tasks remains undiminished. And we of the current generation are determined at least to try and match your own achievements.

23 April 1987

APPENDIX II

Letter to an MP

3 June 1988

House of Commons,
London SW1

Dear ——————,

I am aware of your comments in the media about the Peter Wright case and your general view about the obligations of officers in our Intelligence Services.

Rather than wait for you to make some further comment about me and my book, *Inside Intelligence*, I would like to set out certain facts for you.

I am not aware that you have served either in MI5 or MI6. What information you have, therefore, relating to the terms of service, methods of recruitment and the administration of the Security Service and the Secret Intelligence Service, is second-hand. That is to say, you have been told about them by parties representing them, or the Government which controls them.

I am sorry to say that the line the Government continues to use with regard to myself is untrue.

The Attorney-General and the Treasury Solicitor have both been at pains to contend that officers who have served in either of the Intelligence Services owe the Crown a life-long duty of confidentiality relating to their service.

Richard Norton-Taylor, writing in the *Guardian*, quotes George Kennedy Young, a former Vice Chief of SIS, as saying that up until he left the Service in 1963, the term obligation of confidentiality was unknown. Norton-Taylor contacted a further four former SIS officers, who confirmed this to him. There is no question of the term having been in use, or the obligation having been a part of any understanding between the Service and its officers, when I left in 1953.

My book was not written to make money. As a former officer, loyalty must mean something to you. It does to me, and I was not prepared to see my old boss, both in the Army and in SIS, smeared. I told SIS I was

175

writing a book and I submitted it to them. They said nothing I had written could be published.

I published privately, and subsequently in the Courts two-thirds of the book was freed from the Injunction, including all of that part relating to my service in MI5.

The blue pencilling, to say the least, was arbitrary and, in many cases, without logic.

Kim Philby's recent death reminds us that the paperwork and administration of the intelligence services, during and at the end of the war, was not efficient. It is clear now that Philby was never properly vetted. Similarly, other people who had been members of the Communist Party or practising homosexuals were recruited into the Service without difficulty. There was certainly no agreement of employment and no undertaking was given, other than that required by the signing of the relevant portions of the Official Secrets Act.

The Attorney General has stated more than once, that the Government in no way contends that I have breached the Official Secrets Act. That being so, and not having given any undertaking of confidentiality, it is clear that the injunctions that have been taken out against newspapers to prevent them quoting anything I have said, are no more than a gagging procedure. The next step, as you know, is the Appeal to the House of Lords, which will be heard in the autumn.

Sir Dick White, when he took over as Chief of SIS, started to put his house in order, and officers who left the Service after his arrival, were required to sign a 'supplementary declaration', in which they undertook to do nothing which would be to the detriment of the Service, at the risk of losing their superannuation rights.

I have not made a penny out of the publication of *Inside Intelligence*. Indeed, it has cost me approaching £5000. Several thousand pounds, which newspapers were willing to pay me, I directed to Century House Benevolent Fund. They have, however, rejected the money. I shall no doubt be able to find an ex-Services charity which is more sensibly run.

I hope you will find time to read this. You seem to be a regular commentator on intelligence matters, and I would like to know when I listen to you or read what you have said in future, that you knew the facts.

I am sending copies of this letter to Tam Dalyell and Richard Shepherd, who are both interested in this saga.

ANTHONY CAVENDISH

INDEX

mercenary, 3, 4
  motives, 3
intelligence operatives
  covers used by, 77, 78, 79
  ranks, 78
Intourist, 80
Iran
  coup, 139–40
Iraq, King of
  assassinated, 120
Isham, Sir Gyles, 20, 135, 136
ISLD (Inter Services Liaison
  Department), 18
Ismailia, 29, 30, 31, 32
IZL (Irqun Zvai Leumi), 17, 19, 21
  hangs British Sergeants, 22
Izzard, Ralph, 137

Jacobs, Joe, 108
Jedrychowski, Stefan, 107
Jerusalem, 18

Karamanlis, Konstantine, 123
Kassem, General, 132
Kelly, Grace, 83
Kennedy, John F., 126, 127
Kethly, Anna, 96
Khomeini, Ayatollah, 142
Khoury, Abdulla, 133
Kielmanseg, Colonel Graf Adolf von,
  106
Kindberg, 67
King David Hotel bombing, 18, 19
King's African Rifles, 26
Klose, Lieutenant Commander Hans
  Helmut, 54, 56, 58, 59
Kovacs, General Istvan, 95
Krupp, 123
Kruschev, Nikita, 83, 107, 126, 127,
  137
Kung Peng, 115
Kupi, Abas, 52

League of Free Jurists, 49
Leiser, Ernest, 102
Linse, Walter, 49

Locum, Captain Frank, 36
Lodz, 116
Los Angeles Times, 142
Luce, Sir William, 141

MacKintosh of MacKintosh, Rear
  Admiral the, 55
Macmillan, Harold, 116
Magan, William, 20
Mail on Sunday, 160, 161
Makarios, Archbishop, 119, 122
Maleter, Major General Pal, 95, 97, 99
Malik, Wing Commander Sirdar, 82
Mannesmann, 123
Margaret, HRH Princess, 84
Mariazell, 75
Martin, Sergeant, 23
McLean, Billy, 52
McLean, Donald, 1, 62, 137
McNab, Brigadier Geoffrey, 17
McNee, Sir David, 157
Melburne, Roy, 139
Melk, 67, 68, 69
Mendes-France, Pierre, 83
Menuhin, Diana, 114
Menuhin, Yehudi, 114
Menzies, Major General Sir Stewart, 1,
  39, 51, 137, 149
merchant banks, 79
MI5, 16, 39, 44, 163, 168, 170
  plans to destabilise Wilson
    Government, 164
MI6, 18, 34, 36, 38n, 39, 156, 165
  in Tehran, 141
  structure, 39–40
  typical recruits, 77
MIG-15 Soviet fighter, 44
Miller, James, 168
Milne, Tim, 136
Milne, Tony, 36, 41, 135, 136
Milotinovic, Mirko, 85
Mindszenty, Josef Cardinal, 100
Morris, Joe Alex, 142
Moscow Narody, 80
Mossadeqh, Dr Mohammed, 139, 140
Mulla, Bader Al, 134